日本語能力試験
AF442122
JAPANESE-LANGUAGE
PROFICIENCY TEST
Full N1-N5 Kanji Vocabulary List
Japanese - English - Tamil
Nihongo Tutors has been the most trusted tutoring
institution in the area for over 3 years. We won't fail you!

N5	N5	N5	N5
日	一	国	人
day, sun, Japan	one	country	person
நாள்	ஒன்று	நாடு	நபர்

N5	N5	N5	N5
年	大	十	二
year	large, big	ten	two
ஆண்டு	பெரியது	பத்து	இரண்டு

N5	N5	N5	N5
本	中	長	出
book, present, main, true, real	in, inside, middle, mean, center	long, leader	exit, leave
பிரதான	இல்	நீண்டது	வெளியேறு

N5	N5	N5	N5
三	時	行	見
three	time, hour	going, journey	see, hopes, chances, idea, opinion, look at, visible
மூன்று	நேரம்	போகிறது	பார்க்க

N5	N5	N5	N5
月	後	前	五
month, moon	behind, back, later	in front, before	five
மாதம்	பின்னால்	முன்னால்	ஐந்து

N5	N5	N5	N5
間	上	東	四
interval, space	above, up	east	four
இடைவெளி	மேலே	கிழக்கு	நான்கு
今	金	九	入
now	gold	nine	enter, insert
இப்போது	தங்கம்	ஒன்பது	உள்ளிடவும்
学	高	円	子
study, learning, science	tall, high, expensive	circle, yen, round	child, sign of the rat, 11PM-1AM
படிப்பு	உயரமான	வட்டம்	குழந்தை
外	八	六	下
outside	eight	six	below, down, descend, give, low, inferior
வெளியே	எட்டு	ஆறு	கீழே
来	気	小	七
come, due, next, cause, become	spirit, mind	little, small	seven
வாருங்கள்	ஆவி	சிறிய	ஏழு

山 N5	話 N5	女 N5	北 N5
mountain	tale, talk	woman, female	north
மலை	கதை	பெண்	வடக்கு
午 N5	百 N5	書 N5	先 N5
noon, sign of the horse, 11AM-1PM	hundred	write	before, ahead, previous, future, precedence
நண்பகல்	நூறு	எழுதுங்கள்	முன்,
名 N5	川 N5	千 N5	水 N5
name, noted, distinguished, reputation	stream, river	thousand	water
பெயர்	ஸ்ட்ரீம், நதி	ஆயிரம்	தண்ணீர்
半 N5	男 N5	西 N5	電 N5
half, middle, odd number, semi-, part-half	male	west, Spain	electricity
பாதி	ஆண்	மேற்கு	மின்சாரம்
校 N5	語 N5	土 N5	木 N5
exam, school, printing, proof, correction	word, speech, language	soil, earth, ground, Turkey	tree, wood
தேர்வு	சொல்	மண்	மரம்

N5	N5	N5	N5
聞	食	車	何
hear, ask, listen	eat, food	car	what
கேள்	சாப்பிடுங்கள்	கார்	என்ன
N5	N5	N5	N5
南	万	毎	白
south	ten thousand	every	white
தெற்கு	பத்தாயிரம்	ஒவ்வொன்றும்	வெள்ளை
N5	N5	N5	N5
天	母	火	右
heavens, sky, imperial	mama, mother	fire	right
வானம்	அம்மா	தீ	சரி
N5	N5	N5	N5
読	友	左	休
read	friend	left	rest, day off, retire, sleep
படி	நண்பர்	இடது	ஓய்வு
N5	N5	N5	N5
父	雨	会	同
father	rain	meeting, meet, party, association, interview, join	same, agree, equal
அப்பா	மழை	சந்தித்தல்	அதே

N4	N4	N4	N4
事	**自**	**社**	**発**
matter, thing, fact, business, reason, possibly	oneself	company, firm, office, association, shrine	discharge, departure, publish, emit, start from
விஷயம்	தன்னை	நிறுவனம்	வெளியேற்றம்

N4	N4	N4	N4
者	**地**	**業**	**方**
someone, person	ground, earth	business, vocation, arts, performance	direction, person, alternative
யாரோ	தரையில்	வணிக	திசையில்

N4	N4	N4	N4
新	**場**	**員**	**立**
new	location, place	employee, member, number, the one in charge	stand up
புதியது	இடம்	ஊழியர்	எழுந்து நில்

N4	N4	N4	N4
開	**手**	**力**	**問**
open, unfold, unseal	hand	power, strong, strain, bear up, exert	question, ask, problem
திறந்த	கை	வலுவான	கேள்வி

N4	N4	N4	N4
代	**明**	**動**	**京**
substitute, change, convert, replace, period	bright, light	move, motion, change, confusion, shift, shake	capital
மாற்று	பிரகாசமான	நகர்வு	மூலதனம்

目 (N4)	通 (N4)	言 (N4)	理 (N4)
eye, class, look, insight, experience, care, favor	traffic, pass through, avenue, commute	say	logic, arrangement, reason, justice, truth
கண்	போக்குவரத்து	சொல்	தர்க்கம்
体 (N4)	田 (N4)	主 (N4)	題 (N4)
body, substance, object, reality, counter for images	rice field, rice paddy	lord, chief, master, main thing, principal	topic, subject
உடல்	நெல் வயல்	ஆண்டவர்	தலைப்பு
意 (N4)	不 (N4)	作 (N4)	用 (N4)
idea, mind, heart, taste, thought, desire	negative, non-, bad, ugly, clumsy	make, production, prepare, build	utilize, business, service, use, employ
யோசனை	எதிர்மறை	செய்ய	பயன்படுத்த
度 (N4)	強 (N4)	公 (N4)	持 (N4)
degrees, occurrence, time, counter for occurrences	strong	public, prince, official, governmental	hold, have
டிகிரி	வலுவான	பொது	பிடி
野 (N4)	以 (N4)	思 (N4)	家 (N4)
plains, field, rustic, civilian life	by means of, because, in view of, compared with	think	house, home
சமவெளி	ஏனெனில்	சிந்தியுங்கள்	வீடு

世 N4	多 N4	正 N4	院 N4
generation, world, society, public	many, frequent, much	correct, justice, righteous, 10**40	Inst., institution, temple, mansion, school
தலைமுறை	நிறைய	சரி	மாளிகை
心 N4	界 N4	教 N4	文 N4
heart, mind, spirit	world	teach, faith, doctrine	sentence, literature, style, art, decoration
இதயம்	உலகம்	கற்பித்தல்	தண்டனை
元 N4	重 N4	近 N4	考 N4
beginning, former time, origin	heavy, heap up, pile up, nest of boxes, -fold	near, early, akin, tantamount	consider, think over
ஆரம்பம்	கனமான	அருகில்	கருத்தில் கொள்ளுங்கள்
画 N4	海 N4	売 N4	知 N4
brush-stroke, picture	sea, ocean	sell	know, wisdom
படம்	கடல்	விற்க	தெரியும்
道 N4	集 N4	別 N4	物 N4
road-way, street, district, journey, course	gather, meet, congregate, swarm, flock	separate, branch off, diverge, fork, another	thing, object, matter
தெரு	சேகரிக்க	தனி	விஷயம்

使 N4 use பயன்பாடு	**品** N4 goods, refinement, dignity, article பொருட்கள்	**計** N4 plot, plan, scheme, measure சதி	**死** N4 death, die இறப்பு
特 N4 special சிறப்பு	**私** N4 private, I, me தனிப்பட்ட	**始** N4 commence, begin தொடங்குங்கள்	**朝** N4 morning, dynasty, regime, epoch, period காலை
運 N4 carry, luck, destiny, fate, lot, transport எடுத்துச் செல்லுங்கள்	**終** N4 end, finish முடிவு	**台** N4 pedestal, a stand, counter for machines and vehicles பீடம்	**広** N4 wide, broad, spacious பரந்த
住 N4 dwell, reside, live, inhabit வாழ	**真** N4 true, reality, Buddhist sect உண்மை	**有** N4 possess, have, exist, happen, occur, approx வைத்திருங்கள்	**口** N4 mouth வாய்
少 N4 few, little சில	**町** N4 village, town, block, street கிராமம்	**料** N4 fee, materials கட்டணம்	**工** N4 craft, construction கைவினை

建 N4	空 N4	急 N4	止 N4
build	empty, sky, void, vacant, vacuum	hurry, emergency, sudden, steep	stop, halt
கட்ட	காலியாக	அவசரம்	நிறுத்து
送 N4	切 N4	転 N4	研 N4
escort, send	cut, cutoff, be sharp	revolve, turn around, change	polish, study of, sharpen
துணை	வெட்டு	சுற்றவும்	போலிஷ்
足 N4	究 N4	楽 N4	起 N4
leg, foot, be sufficient	research, study	music, comfort, ease	rouse, wake up, get up
கால்	ஆராய்ச்சி	இசை	எழு
着 N4	店 N4	病 N4	質 N4
arrive, wear, counter for suits of clothing	store, shop	ill, sick	substance, quality, matter, temperament
வந்து சேருங்கள்	கடை	நோய்வாய்ப்பட்டது	பொருள்
待 N4	試 N4	族 N4	銀 N4
wait, depend on	test, try, attempt, experiment, ordeal	tribe, family	silver
காத்திரு	சோதனை	பழங்குடி	வெள்ளி

早 N4 early, fast ஆரம்ப	**映** N4 reflect, reflection, projection பிரதிபலிக்கவும்	**親** N4 parent, intimacy, relative, familiarity பெற்றோர்	**験** N4 verification, effect, testing சரிபார்ப்பு
英 N4 England, English இங்கிலாந்து	**医** N4 doctor, medicine மருத்துவர்	**仕** N4 attend, doing, official, serve கலந்து கொள்ளுங்கள்	**去** N4 gone, past, quit, leave, elapse, eliminate, divorce போய்விட்டது
味 N4 flavor, taste சுவை	**写** N4 copy, be photographed, describe நகல்	**字** N4 character, letter, word, section of village தன்மை	**答** N4 solution, answer தீர்வு
夜 N4 night, evening இரவு	**音** N4 sound, noise ஒலி	**注** N4 pour, irrigate, shed (tears), flow into ஊற்றவும்	**帰** N4 homecoming, arrive at, lead to, result in வீடு திரும்புவது
古 N4 old பழையது	**歌** N4 song, sing பாடல்	**買** N4 buy வாங்க	**悪** N4 bad, vice, rascal, false, evil, wrong மோசமான

Kanji	English	Tamil
図 (N4)	map, drawing, plan, unexpected, accidentally	வரைபடம்
週 (N4)	week	வாரம்
室 (N4)	room, apartment, chamber, greenhouse, cellar	அறை
歩 (N4)	walk, counter for steps	நட
風 (N4)	wind, air, style, manner	காற்று
紙 (N4)	paper	காகிதம்
黒 (N4)	black	கருப்பு
花 (N4)	flower	பூ
春 (N4)	springtime, spring (season)	வசந்த காலம்
赤 (N4)	red	சிவப்பு
青 (N4)	blue, green	நீலம்
館 (N4)	building, mansion, large building, palace	கட்டிடம்
屋 (N4)	roof, house, shop, dealer, seller	கூரை
色 (N4)	color	நிறம்
走 (N4)	run	ஓடு
秋 (N4)	autumn	இலையுதிர் காலம்
夏 (N4)	summer	கோடை
習 (N4)	learn	அறிய
駅 (N4)	station	நிலையம்
洋 (N4)	ocean, western style	கடல்

旅 N4	服 N4	夕 N4	借 N4
trip, travel	clothing, admit, obey, discharge	evening	borrow, rent
பயணம்	ஆடை	சாயங்காலம்	கடன் வாங்க
曜 N4	飲 N4	肉 N4	貸 N4
weekday	drink, smoke, take	meat	lend
வார நாள்	பானம்	இறைச்சி	கடன் கொடுங்கள்
堂 N4	鳥 N4	飯 N4	勉 N4
public chamber, hall	bird, chicken	meal, boiled rice	exertion
மண்டபம்	பறவை	உணவு	உழைப்பு
冬 N4	昼 N4	茶 N4	牛 N4
winter	daytime, noon	tea	cow
குளிர்காலம்	பகல்நேரம்	தேநீர்	மாடு
魚 N4	兄 N4	犬 N4	漢 N4
fish	elder brother, big brother	dog	Sino-, China
மீன்	மூத்த அண்ணன்	நாய்	சீனா

政

politics, government

அரசு

議

deliberation, consultation, debate, consideration

கலந்துரையாடல்

民

people, nation, subjects

மக்கள்

連

take along, lead, join, connect, party, gang, clique

உடன் செல்லுங்கள்

対

vis-a-vis, opposite, even, equal, versus, anti-

எதிர்

部

section, bureau, dept, class, copy, part

பிரிவு

合

fit, suit, join

வழக்கு

市

market, city, town

சந்தை

内

inside, within, between, among, house, home

உள்ளே

相

inter-, mutual, together, each other

ஒன்றாக

定

determine, fix, establish, decide

தீர்மானிக்கவும்

回

-times, round, game, revolve

விளையாட்டு

選

elect, select, choose, prefer

ர்ந்தெடுக்கப்பட்டவர்

米

rice, USA, metre

அரிசி

実

reality, truth

உண்மை

関

connection, barrier, gateway, involve, concerning

இணைப்பு

決

decide, fix, agree upon, appoint

முடிவு

全

whole, entire, all, complete, fulfill

முழு

表

surface, table, chart, diagram

மேற்பரப்பு

戦

war, battle, match

போர்

N3	N3	N3	N3
経	最	現	調
sutra, longitude, pass thru, expire, warp	utmost, most, extreme	present, existing, actual	tune, tone, meter, key (music), writing style
தீர்க்கரேகை	மிகவும்	தற்போது	டியூன்
化	当	約	首
change, take the form of, influence, enchant	hit, right, appropriate, himself	promise, approximately, shrink	neck
மாற்றம்	வெற்றி	வாக்குறுதி	கழுத்து
法	性	要	制
method, law, rule, principle, model, system	sex, gender, nature	need, main point, essence, pivot, key to	system, law, rule
முறை	பாலினம்	தேவை	அமைப்பு
治	務	成	期
reign, be at peace, calm down, subdue, quell	task, duties	turn into, become, get, grow, elapse, reach	period, time, date, term
ஆட்சி	பணி	ஆக	காலம்
取	都	和	機
take, fetch, take up	metropolis, capital	harmony, Japanese style, peace, soften, Japan	mechanism, opportunity, occasion, machine, airplane
டுத்துக்கொள்ளுங்க	பெருநகர	நல்லிணக்கம்	பொறிமுறை

N3	N3	N3	N3
平	**加**	**受**	**続**
even, flat, peace	add, addition, increase, join, include, Canada	accept, undergo, answer (phone), take, get	continue, series, sequel
கூட	கூட்டு	ஏற்றுக்கொள்	தொடரவும்
進	**数**	**記**	**初**
advance, proceed, progress, promote	number, strength, fate, law, figures	scribe, account, narrative	first time, beginning
முன்கூட்டியே	எண்	எழுத்தாளர்	ஆரம்பம்
指	**権**	**支**	**産**
finger, point to, indicate, put into, play (chess)	authority, power, rights	branch, support, sustain	products, bear, give birth, yield, childbirth
விரல்	அதிகாரம்	கிளை	தயாரிப்புகள்
点	**報**	**済**	**活**
spot, point, mark, speck, decimal point	report, news, reward, retribution	finish, come to an end, excusable, need not	lively, resuscitation, being helped, living
ஸ்பாட்	அறிக்கை	பூச்சு	கலகலப்பான
原	**共**	**得**	**解**
meadow, original, primitive, field, plain	together, both, neither, all, and, alike, with	gain, get, find, earn, acquire, can, may	unravel, notes, key, explanation
புல்வெளி	ஒன்றாக	ஆதாயம்	அவிழ்த்து விடுங்கள்

N3 交	N3 資	N3 予	N3 向
mingle, mixing, association, coming & going	assets, resources, capital, funds, data	beforehand, previous, myself, I	yonder, facing, beyond, confront, defy
கலத்தல்	சொத்துக்கள்	முன்பே	யோண்டர்
N3 際	N3 勝	N3 面	N3 告
occasion, side, edge, verge, dangerous, adventurous	victory, win, prevail, excel	mask, face, features, surface	revelation, tell, inform, announce
விழாவில்	வெற்றி	முகமூடி	வெளிப்பாடு
N3 反	N3 判	N3 認	N3 参
anti-	judgement, signature, stamp, seal	acknowledge, witness, discern, recognize	nonplussed, three, going, coming, visiting
எதிர்ப்பு	தீர்ப்பு	ஒப்புக்கொள்	nonplussed
N3 利	N3 組	N3 信	N3 在
profit, advantage, benefit	association, braid, plait, construct, assemble	faith, truth, fidelity, trust	exist, outskirts, suburbs, located in
லாபம்	சங்கம்	நம்பிக்கை	உள்ளன
N3 件	N3 側	N3 任	N3 引
affair, case, matter, item	side, lean, oppose, regret	responsibility, duty, term, entrust to, appoint	pull, tug, jerk, admit, install, quote, refer to
விவகாரம்	பக்க	பொறுப்பு	இழுக்கவும்

求 N3	所 N3	次 N3	昨 N3
request, want, wish for, require, demand	place	next, order, sequence	yesterday, previous
கோரிக்கை	இடம்	அடுத்தது	நேற்று
論 N3	官 N3	増 N3	係 N3
argument, discourse	bureaucrat, the government	increase, add, augment, gain, promote	person in charge, connection, duty, concern oneself
வாதம்	அதிகாரத்துவம்	அதிகரி	கடமை
感 N3	情 N3	投 N3	示 N3
emotion, feeling, sensation	feelings, emotion, passion, sympathy	throw, discard, abandon, launch into, join	show, indicate, point out, express, display
உணர்ச்சி	உணர்வுகள்	வீசு	காட்டு
変 N3	打 N3	直 N3	両 N3
unusual, change, strange	strike, hit, knock, pound, dozen	straightaway, honesty, frankness, fix, repair	both, old Japanese coin, counter for vehicles, two
அசாதாரணமானது	வேலைநிறுத்தம்	நேராக	இரண்டும்
式 N3	確 N3	果 N3	容 N3
style, ceremony, rite, function, method, system	assurance, firm, tight, hard, solid, confirm	fruit, reward, carry out, achieve, complete, end	contain, form, looks
நடை	உறுதி	வெகுமதி	கொண்டிருக்கும்

必 (N3)	演 (N3)	歳 (N3)	争 (N3)
invariably, certain, inevitable	performance, act, play, render, stage	year-end, age, occasion, opportunity	contend, dispute, argue
மாறாமல்	செயல்திறன்	விழாவில்	சண்டை
談 (N3)	能 (N3)	位 (N3)	置 (N3)
discuss, talk	ability, talent, skill, capacity	rank, grade, throne, crown, about, some	placement, put, set, deposit, leave behind
விவாதிக்க	திறன்	ரேங்க்	வேலை வாய்ப்பு
流 (N3)	格 (N3)	疑 (N3)	過 (N3)
current, a sink, flow, forfeit	status, rank, capacity, character	doubt, distrust, be suspicious, question	overdo, exceed, go beyond, error
தற்போதைய	நிலை	சந்தேகம்	மிகை
局 (N3)	放 (N3)	常 (N3)	状 (N3)
bureau, board, office, affair, conclusion	set free, release, fire, shoot, emit, banish	usual, ordinary, normal, regular	status quo, conditions, circumstances, form
பணியகம்	வெளியீடு	வழக்கம்	நிபந்தனைகள்
球 (N3)	職 (N3)	与 (N3)	供 (N3)
ball, sphere	post, employment, work	bestow, participate in, give, award, impart, provide	submit, offer, present, serve (meal), accompany
பந்து	அஞ்சல்	சிறந்த	சமர்ப்பிக்கவும்

役 N3 duty, war, campaign, drafted labor, office, service கடமை	**構** N3 posture, build, pretend தோரணை	**割** N3 proportion, comparatively, divide, cut, separate விகிதம்	**費** N3 expense, cost, spend, consume, waste செலவு
付 N3 adhere, attach, refer to, append பின்பற்றுங்கள்	**由** N3 wherefore, a reason எனவே	**説** N3 rumor, opinion, theory வதந்தி	**難** N3 difficult, impossible, trouble, accident, defect கடினம்
優 N3 tenderness, excel, surpass, actor, superiority மென்மை	**夫** N3 husband, man கணவர்	**収** N3 income, obtain, reap, pay, supply, store வருமானம்	**断** N3 severance, decline, refuse, apologize பிரித்தல்
石 N3 stone கல்	**違** N3 difference, differ வித்தியாசம்	**消** N3 extinguish, blow out, turn off, neutralize, cancel அணை	**神** N3 gods, mind, soul தெய்வங்கள்
番 N3 turn, number in a series திரும்பவும்	**規** N3 standard, measure தரநிலை	**術** N3 art, technique, skill, means, trick, resources கலை	**備** N3 equip, provision, preparation சித்தப்படுத்துங்கள்

宅 N3 home, house, residence, our house, my husband வீடு	**害** N3 harm, injury தீங்கு	**配** N3 distribute, spouse, exile, rationing விநியோகிக்கவும்	**警** N3 admonish, commandment அறிவுறுத்துங்கள்
育 N3 bring up, grow up, raise, rear உயர்த்த	**席** N3 seat, mat, occasion, place இருக்கை	**訪** N3 call on, visit, look up, offer sympathy வருகை	**乗** N3 ride, power, multiplication, record சவாரி
残 N3 remainder, leftover, balance மீதமுள்ள	**想** N3 concept, think, idea, thought கருத்து	**声** N3 voice குரல்	**念** N3 wish, sense, idea, thought, feeling, desire விரும்பும்
助 N3 help, rescue, assist உதவி	**労** N3 labor, thank for, reward for, toil, trouble தொழிலாளர்	**例** N3 example, custom, usage, precedent உதாரணமாக	**然** N3 sort of thing, so, if so, in that case, well அதனால்
限 N3 limit, restrict, to best of ability அளவு	**追** N3 chase, drive away, follow, pursue, meanwhile துரத்து	**商** N3 make a deal, selling, dealing in, merchant விற்பனை	**葉** N3 leaf, plane, lobe, needle, blade, spear இலை

N3	N3	N3	N3
伝 transmit, go along, walk along, follow, report கடத்து	**働** work, (kokuji) வேலை	**形** shape, form, style வடிவம்	**景** scenery, view இயற்கைக்காட்சி
好 fond, pleasing, like something பிடிக்கும்	**退** retreat, withdraw, retire, resign, repel, expel பின்வாங்குதல்	**頭** head, counter for large animals தலை	**負** defeat, negative, -, minus, bear, owe தோல்வி
渡 transit, ford, ferry, cross, import, deliver போக்குவரத்து	**失** lose, error, fault, disadvantage, loss இழக்க	**差** distinction, difference, variation, discrepancy வேறுபாடு	**末** end, close, tip, powder, posterity முடிவு
守 guard, protect, defend, obey காவலர்	**若** young, if, perhaps, possibly, low number, immature இளம்	**種** species, kind, class, variety, seed இனங்கள்	**美** beauty, beautiful அழகு
命 fate, command, decree, destiny, life, appoint விதி	**福** blessing, fortune, luck, wealth ஆசீர்வாதம்	**望** ambition, full moon, hope, desire, aspire to, expect லட்சியம்	**非** un-, mistake, negative, injustice, non- எதிர்மறை

観 N3	察 N3	段 N3	横 N3
outlook, look, appearance, condition, view	guess, presume, surmise, judge, understand	grade, steps, stairs	sideways, side, horizontal, width, woof
கண்ணோட்டம்	யூகம்	தரம்	பக்கவாட்டாக
深 N3	申 N3	様 N3	財 N3
deep, heighten, intensify, strengthen	have the honor to, sign of the monkey, 3-5PM	Esq., way, manner, situation, polite suffix	property, money, wealth, assets
ஆழமான	மரியாதை வேண்டும்	முறை	சொத்து
港 N3	識 N3	呼 N3	達 N3
harbor	discriminating, know, write	call, call out to, invite	accomplished, reach, arrive, attain
துறைமுகம்	பாகுபாடு காண்பித்தல்	அழைப்பு	நிறைவேற்றப்பட்டது
良 N3	候 N3	程 N3	満 N3
good, pleasing, skilled	climate, season, weather	extent, degree, law, formula, distance, limits	full, enough, pride, satisfy
நல்ல	காலநிலை	அளவு	முழு
敗 N3	値 N3	光 N3	路 N3
failure, defeat, reversal	price, cost, value	ray, light	path, route, road, distance
தோல்வி	விலை	கதிர்	பாதை

科 N3	積 N3	他 N3	処 N3
department, course, section	volume, product (x*y), acreage, contents, pile up	other, another, the others	dispose, manage, deal with, sentence, condemn
துறை	தொகுதி	மற்றவை	அப்புறப்படுத்து
太 N3	客 N3	否 N3	師 N3
plump, thick, big around	guest, visitor, customer, client	negate, no, noes, refuse, decline, deny	expert, teacher, master, army, war
குண்டாக	விருந்தினர்	மறுக்க	நிபுணர்
登 N3	易 N3	速 N3	存 N3
ascend, climb up	easy, ready to, simple, fortune-telling, divination	quick, fast	suppose, be aware of, believe, feel
ஏறு	சுலபம்	விரைவான	நினைக்கிறேன்
飛 N3	殺 N3	号 N3	単 N3
fly, skip (pages), scatter	kill, murder, butcher, slice off, split, diminish	nickname, number, item, title, pseudonym, name, call	simple, one, single, merely
சிதறல்	கொல்ல	புனைப்பெயர்	எளிய
座 N3	破 N3	除 N3	完 N3
squat, seat, cushion, gathering, sit	rend, rip, tear, break, destroy, defeat, frustrate	exclude, division (x, 3), remove, abolish, cancel	perfect, completion, end
குந்து	ரெண்ட்	விலக்கு	சரியானது

降 N3 descend, precipitate, fall, surrender இறங்க	**責** N3 blame, condemn, censure பழி	**捕** N3 catch, capture பிடி	**危** N3 dangerous, fear, uneasy ஆபத்தானது
給 N3 salary, wage, gift, allow, grant, bestow on சம்பளம்	**苦** N3 suffering, trial, worry, hardship, feel bitter துன்பம்	**迎** N3 welcome, meet, greet வரவேற்பு	**園** N3 park, garden, yard, farm பூங்கா
具 N3 tool, utensil, means, possess, ingredients கருவி	**辞** N3 resign, word, term, expression ராஜினாமா	**因** N3 cause, factor, be associated with, depend on காரணம்	**馬** N3 horse குதிரை
愛 N3 love, affection, favourite காதல்	**富** N3 wealth, enrich, abundant செல்வம்	**彼** N3 he, that, the அவர்	**未** N3 un-, not yet, hitherto, still, even now இன்னும்
舞 N3 dance, flit, circle, wheel நடனம்	**亡** N3 deceased, the late, dying, perish இறந்தவர்	**冷** N3 cool, cold (beer, person), chill குளிர்	**適** N3 suitable, occasional, rare, qualified, capable பொருத்தமானது

婦 N3	寄 N3	込 N3	顔 N3
lady, woman, wife, bride	draw near, stop in, bring near, gather, collect	crowded, mixture, in bulk, included	face, expression
பெண்	சேகரிக்க	கூட்டம்	வெளிப்பாடு
類 N3	余 N3	王 N3	返 N3
sort, kind, variety, class, genus	too much, myself, surplus, other, remainder	king, rule, magnate	return, answer, fade, repay
வகைபடுத்து	அதிகமாக	ராஜா	திரும்ப
妻 N3	背 N3	熱 N3	宿 N3
wife, spouse	stature, height, back, behind, disobey, defy	heat, temperature, fever, mania, passion	inn, lodging, relay station, dwell, lodge
மனைவி	அந்தஸ்து	வெப்பம்	சத்திரம்
薬 N3	頼 N3	覚 N3	船 N3
medicine, chemical, enamel, gunpowder, benefit	trust, request	memorize, learn, remember, awake, sober up	ship, boat
மருந்து	நம்பிக்கை	மனப்பாடம் செய்யுங்கள்	படகு
途 N3	許 N3	抜 N3	便 N3
route, way, road	permit, approve	slip out, extract, pull out, pilfer, quote, remove	convenience
பாதை	அனுமதி	பிரித்தெடுத்தல்	வசதி

留 N3	罪 N3	努 N3	精 N3
detain, fasten, halt, stop	guilt, sin, crime, fault, blame, offense	toil, diligent, as much as possible	refined, ghost, fairy, energy, vitality, semen
தடுத்து	குற்றம்	விடாமுயற்சி	சுத்திகரிக்கப்பட்டது
散 N3	静 N3	婚 N3	喜 N3
scatter, disperse, spend, squander	quiet	marriage	rejoice, take pleasure in
சிதறல்	அமைதியான	திருமணம்	மகிழ்ச்சியுங்கள்
浮 N3	絶 N3	幸 N3	押 N3
floating, float, rise to surface	discontinue, beyond, sever, cut off, abstain	happiness, blessing, fortune	push, stop, check, subdue, attach
மிதக்கும்	நிறுத்து	மகிழ்ச்சி	மிகுதி
倒 N3	老 N3	曲 N3	払 N3
overthrow, fall, collapse, drop, break down	old man, old age, grow old	bend, music, melody, composition	pay, clear out, prune, banish, dispose of
தூக்கி எறியுங்கள்	வயதாகிவிடும்	வளைவு	செலுத்த
庭 N3	徒 N3	勤 N3	遅 N3
courtyard, garden, yard	junior, emptiness, vanity, futility, uselessness	diligence, become employed, serve	slow, late, back, later
முற்றம்	ஜூனியர்	விடாமுயற்சி	மெதுவாக

Kanji	Meaning	Tamil	Level
居	reside, to be, exist, live with	வசிக்க	N3
雑	miscellaneous	இதர	N3
招	beckon, invite, summon, engage	பெக்கன்	N3
困	quandary, become distressed, annoyed	இரைச்சல்,	N3
刻	engrave, cut fine, chop, hash, mince, time, carving	வேலைப்பாடு	N3
賛	approve, praise, title or inscription on picture	ஒப்புதல்	N3
抱	embrace, hug, hold in arms	தழுவி	N3
犯	crime, sin, offense	குற்றம்	N3
恐	fear, dread, awe	பயம்	N3
息	breath, respiration, son, interest (on money)	மூச்சு	N3
遠	distant, far	தொலைதூர	N3
戻	re-, return, revert, resume, restore, go backwards	மாற்றியமைக்கவும்	N3
願	petition, request, vow, wish, hope	மனு	N3
絵	picture, drawing, painting, sketch	படம்	N3
越	surpass, cross over, move to, exceed, Vietnam	மிஞ்சும்	N3
欲	longing, covetousness, greed, passion, desire	ஏங்குதல்	N3
痛	pain, hurt, damage, bruise	வலி	N3
笑	laugh	சிரிக்கவும்	N3
互	mutually, reciprocally, together	பரஸ்பரம்	N3
束	bundle, sheaf, ream, tie in bundles, govern	மூட்டை	N3

似 N3	列 N3	探 N3	逃 N3
becoming, resemble, counterfeit, imitate, suitable	file, row, rank, tier, column	grope, search, look for	escape, flee, shirk, evade, set free
ஆகிறது	கோப்பு	grope	தப்பிக்க
遊 N3	迷 N3	夢 N3	君 N3
play	astray, be perplexed, in doubt, lost, err, illusion	dream, vision, illusion	old boy, name-suffix
விளையாடு	வழிதவறி	கனவு	பெரிய பையன்
閉 N3	緒 N3	折 N3	草 N3
closed, shut	thong, beginning, inception, end, cord, strap	fold, break, fracture, bend, yield, submit	grass, weeds, herbs, pasture, write, draft
மூடப்பட்டது	தாங்	மடி	புல்
暮 N3	酒 N3	悲 N3	晴 N3
livelihood, make a living, spend time	sake, alcohol	jail cell, grieve, sad, deplore, regret	clear up
வாழ்வாதாரம்	நிமித்தம்	சிறை	அழிக்கவும்
掛 N3	到 N3	寝 N3	暗 N3
hang, suspend, depend, arrive at, tax, pour	arrival, proceed, reach, attain, result in	lie down, sleep, rest, bed, remain unsold	darkness, disappear, shade, informal
செயலிழக்க	வருகை	தூங்கு	இருள்

Kanji	Meaning	Tamil
盗	steal, rob, pilfer	திருட
吸	suck, imbibe, inhale, sip	சக்
陽	sunshine, yang principle, positive, male, heaven	சூரிய ஒளி
御	honorable, manipulate, govern	க .ரவமான
歯	tooth, cog	பல்
忘	forget	மறந்து விடுங்கள்
雪	snow	பனி
吹	blow, breathe, puff, emit, smoke	அடி
娘	daughter, girl	மகள்
誤	mistake, err, do wrong, mislead	தவறு
洗	wash, inquire into, probe	கழுவுதல்
慣	accustomed, get used to, become experienced	பழக்கமாகிவிட்டது
礼	salute, bow, ceremony, thanks, remuneration	வணக்கம்
窓	window, pane	ஜன்னல்
昔	once upon a time, antiquity, old times	பழங்கால
貧	poverty, poor	வறுமை
怒	angry, be offended	கோபம்
泳	swim	நீந்த
祖	ancestor, pioneer, founder	மூதாதையர்
杯	counter for cupfuls, wine glass, glass, toast	கண்ணாடி

N3	N3	N3	N3
疲	**皆**	**腹**	**煙**
exhausted, tire, weary	all, everything	abdomen, belly, stomach	smoke
தீர்ந்துவிட்டது	எல்லாம்	அடிவயிறு	புகை
眠	**怖**	**耳**	**頂**
sleep, die, sleepy	dreadful, be frightened, fearful	ear	place on the head, receive, top of head, top, summit
தூங்கு	பயங்கரமான	காது	மேல்
箱	**晩**	**寒**	**髪**
box, chest, case, bin, railway car	nightfall, night	cold	hair of the head
பெட்டி	இரவு வீழ்ச்சி	குளிர்	முடி
忙	**才**	**靴**	**恥**
busy, occupied, restless	genius, years old, cubic shaku	shoes	shame, dishonor
பரபரப்பு	மேதை	காலணிகள்	அவமானம்
偶	**偉**	**猫**	**幾**
accidentally, even number, couple, man & wife	admirable, greatness, remarkable, conceited	cat	how many, how much, how far, how long
தற்செயலாக	போற்றத்தக்கது	பூனை	எத்தனை

党 [N2]	協 [N2]	総 [N2]	区 [N2]
party, faction, clique	co-, cooperation	general, whole, all, full, total	ward, district
கட்சி	ஒத்துழைப்பு	பொது	வார்டு
領 [N2]	県 [N2]	設 [N2]	改 [N2]
jurisdiction, dominion, territory, fief, reign	prefecture	establishment, provision, prepare	reformation, change, modify, mend, renew
அதிகார வரம்பு	ப்ரிபெக்சர்	ஸ்தாபனம்	சீர்திருத்தம்
府 [N2]	査 [N2]	委 [N2]	軍 [N2]
borough, urban prefecture, govt office	investigate	committee, entrust to, leave to, devote, discard	army, force, troops, war, battle
பெருநகர	விசாரணை	குழு	இராணுவம்
団 [N2]	各 [N2]	島 [N2]	革 [N2]
group, association	each, every, either	island	leather, become serious, skin, hide, pelt
குழு	ஒவ்வொன்றும்	தீவு	தோல்
村 [N2]	勢 [N2]	減 [N2]	再 [N2]
town, village	forces, energy, military strength	dwindle, decrease, reduce, decline, curtail	again, twice, second time
நகரம்	படைகள்	குறைந்து	மீண்டும்

税 (N2)	営 (N2)	比 (N2)	防 (N2)
tax, duty	occupation, camp, perform, build, conduct (business)	compare, race, ratio, Philipines	ward off, defend, protect, resist
வரி	தொழில்	ஒப்பிடுக	பாதுகாக்க

補 (N2)	境 (N2)	導 (N2)	副 (N2)
supplement, supply, make good, offset, compensate	boundary, border, region	guidance, leading, conduct, usher	vice-, duplicate, copy
துணை	எல்லை	வழிகாட்டல்	நகல்

算 (N2)	輸 (N2)	述 (N2)	線 (N2)
calculate, divining, number, abacus, probability	transport, send, be inferior	mention, state, speak, relate	line, track
கணக்கிடுங்கள்	போக்குவரத்து	குறிப்பிடவும்	டிராக்

農 (N2)	州 (N2)	武 (N2)	象 (N2)
agriculture, farmers	state, province	warrior, military, chivalry, arms	elephant, pattern after, imitate, image, shape
வேளாண்மை	நிலை	போர்வீரன்	யானை

域 (N2)	額 (N2)	欧 (N2)	担 (N2)
range, region, limits, stage, level	forehead, tablet, plaque, framed picture, sum	Europe	shouldering, carry, raise, bear
சரகம்	நெற்றியில்	ஐரோப்பா	தோள்பட்டை

準 N2	**賞** N2	**辺** N2	**造** N2
semi-, correspond to, proportionate to, conform	prize, reward, praise	environs, boundary, border, vicinity	create, make, structure, physique
இணங்க	பரிசு	சுற்றுப்புறங்கள்	உருவாக்கு
被 N2	**技** N2	**低** N2	**復** N2
incur, cover, veil, brood over, shelter, wear	skill, art, craft, ability, feat, performance	lower, short, humble	restore, return to, revert, resume
incur	திறன்	கீழ்	மீட்டமை
移 N2	**個** N2	**門** N2	**課** N2
shift, move, change, drift, catch (cold, fire)	individual, counter for articles and military units	gates	chapter, lesson, section, department, division
மாற்றம்	தனிப்பட்ட	வாயில்கள்	அத்தியாயம்
脳 N2	**極** N2	**含** N2	**蔵** N2
brain, memory	poles, settlement, conclusion, end	include, bear in mind, understand, cherish	storehouse, hide, own, have, possess
மூளை	துருவங்கள்	சேர்க்கிறது	களஞ்சியசாலை
量 N2	**型** N2	**況** N2	**針** N2
quantity, measure, weight, amount, consider	mould, type, model	condition, situation	needle, pin, staple, stinger
அளவு	அச்சு	நிலை	ஊசி

専 N2 specialty, exclusive, mainly, solely சிறப்பு	**谷** N2 valley பள்ளத்தாக்கு	**史** N2 history, chronicle வரலாறு	**階** N2 storey, stair, counter for storeys of a building மாடி
管 N2 pipe, tube, wind instrument, drunken talk குழாய்	**兵** N2 soldier, private, troops, army, warfare, strategy சிப்பாய்	**接** N2 touch, contact, adjoin, piece together தொடு	**細** N2 dainty, get thin, taper, slender, narrow அழகானது
効 N2 merit, efficacy, efficiency, benefit தகுதி	**丸** N2 round, full, month, perfection, -ship, pills சுற்று	**湾** N2 gulf, bay, inlet வளைகுடா	**録** N2 record பதிவு
省 N2 focus, government ministry, conserve கவனம்	**橋** N2 bridge பாலம்	**岸** N2 beach கடற்கரை	**周** N2 circumference, circuit, lap சுற்றளவு
材 N2 lumber, log, timber, wood, talent மரம் வெட்டுதல்	**戸** N2 door கதவு	**央** N2 center, middle மையம்	**券** N2 ticket டிக்கெட்

N2	N2	N2	N2
編	**搜**	**竹**	**並**
compilation, knit, plait, braid, twist, editing	search, look for, locate	bamboo	row, and, besides, as well as, line up, rank with
தொகுப்பு	தேடல்	மூங்கில்	வரிசை
療	**採**	**森**	**競**
heal, cure	pick, take, fetch, take up	forest, woods	emulate, compete with, bid, sell at auction
குணமடைய	பெறு	காடு	பின்பற்றவும்
介	**根**	**販**	**歴**
jammed in, shellfish, mediate, concern oneself with	root, radical, head (pimple)	marketing, sell, trade	curriculum, continuation, passage of time
மட்டி	வேர்	சந்தைப்படுத்தல்	பாடத்திட்டம்
将	**幅**	**般**	**貿**
leader, commander, general, admiral, or	hanging scroll, width	carrier, carry, all	trade, exchange
தலைவர்	அகலம்	கேரியர்	வர்த்தகம்
講	**林**	**裝**	**諸**
lecture, club, association	grove, forest	attire, dress, pretend, disguise, profess	various, many, several, together
சொற்பொழிவு	தோப்பு	உடை	பல்வேறு

N2	N2	N2	N2
劇	河	航	鉄
drama, play	river	navigate, sail, cruise, fly	iron
நாடகம்	நதி	செல்லவும்	இரும்பு
児	禁	印	逆
newborn babe, child, young of animals	prohibition, ban, forbid	stamp, seal, mark, imprint, symbol, emblem	inverted, reverse, opposite, wicked
குழந்தை	தடை	முத்திரை	தலைகீழ்
換	久	短	油
interchange, period, charge, change?	long time, old story	short, brevity, fault, defect, weak point	oil, fat
பரிமாற்றம்	நீண்ட நேரம்	குறுகிய	எண்ணெய்
暴	輪	占	植
outburst, rave, fret, force, violence, cruelty	wheel, ring, circle, link, loop	fortune-telling, divining, forecasting, occupy	plant
வெடிப்பு	சக்கரம்	ஆக்கிரமிக்க	ஆலை
清	倍	均	億
pure, purify, cleanse, exorcise, Manchu dynasty	double, twice, times, fold	level, average	hundred million
தூய்மையானது	இரட்டை	நிலை	பத்து கோடி

Kanji	Meaning	Tamil
圧 (N2)	pressure, push, overwhelm, oppress, dominate	அழுத்தம்
芸 (N2)	technique, art, craft, performance, acting	நுட்பம்
署 (N2)	signature, govt office, police station	கையொப்பம்
伸 (N2)	expand, stretch, extend, lengthen, increase	விரிவாக்கு
停 (N2)	halt, stopping	நிறுத்த
爆 (N2)	bomb, burst open, pop, split	குண்டு
陸 (N2)	land, six	நில
玉 (N2)	jewel, ball	நகை
波 (N2)	waves, billows, Poland	அலைகள்
帯 (N2)	sash, belt, obi, zone, region	சாஷ்
延 (N2)	prolong, stretching	நீடிக்க
羽 (N2)	feathers, counter for birds, rabbits	இறகுகள்
固 (N2)	harden, set, clot, curdle	கடினப்படுத்துங்கள்
則 (N2)	rule, follow, based on, model after	ஆட்சி
乱 (N2)	riot, war, disorder, disturb	கலவரம்
普 (N2)	universal, wide(ly), generally, Prussia	உலகளாவிய
測 (N2)	fathom, plan, scheme, measure	ஆழம்
豊 (N2)	bountiful, excellent, rich	ஏராளமான
厚 (N2)	thick, heavy, rich, kind, cordial, brazen, shameless	அடர்த்தியான
齢 (N2)	age	வயது

囲 N2	卒 N2	略 N2	承 N2
surround, besiege, store, paling, enclosure	graduate, soldier, private, die	abbreviation, omission, outline, shorten, capture	acquiesce, hear, listen to, be informed, receive
சுற்றி	பட்டதாரி	சுருக்கம்	ஏற்றுக்கொள்
順 N2	岩 N2	練 N2	軽 N2
obey, order, turn, right, docility, occasion	boulder, rock, cliff	practice, gloss, train, drill, polish, refine	lightly, trifling, unimportant
கீழ்ப்படியுங்கள்	கற்பாறை	பயிற்சி	லேசாக
了 N2	庁 N2	城 N2	患 N2
complete, finish	government office	castle	afflicted, disease, suffer from, be ill
முழுமை	அரசாங்க அலுவலகம்	கோட்டை	பாதிக்கப்பட்ட
層 N2	版 N2	令 N2	角 N2
stratum, social class, layer, story, floor	printing block, printing plate, edition, impression	orders, ancient laws, command, decree	angle, corner, square, horn, antlers
அடுக்கு	எண்ணம்	ஆர்டர்கள்	கோணம்
絡 N2	損 N2	募 N2	裏 N2
entwine, coil around, get caught in	damage, loss, disadvantage, hurt, injure	recruit, campaign, gather (contributions)	back, amidst, in, reverse, inside, palm, sole
entwine	சேதம்	ஆட்சேர்ப்பு	இடையில்

仏 N2 Buddha, the dead, France புத்தர்	**績** N2 exploits, unreeling cocoons சுரண்டல்கள்	**築** N2 fabricate, build, construct புனையவும்	**貨** N2 freight, goods, property சரக்கு
混 N2 mix, blend, confuse கலவை	**昇** N2 rise up எழுந்திரு	**池** N2 pond, cistern, pool, reservoir குளம்	**血** N2 blood இரத்தம்
温 N2 warm சூடான	**季** N2 seasons பருவங்கள்	**星** N2 star, spot, dot, mark நட்சத்திரம்	**永** N2 eternity, long, lengthy நித்தியம்
著 N2 renowned, publish, write, remarkable புகழ்பெற்றவர்	**誌** N2 document, records ஆவணம்	**庫** N2 warehouse, storehouse கிடங்கு	**刊** N2 publish, carve, engrave வெளியிடு
像 N2 statue, picture, image, figure, portrait சிலை	**香** N2 incense, smell, perfume தூப	**坂** N2 slope, incline, hill சாய்வு	**底** N2 bottom, sole, depth, bottom price, base, kind, sort கீழே

N2	N2	N2	N2
布 linen, cloth கைத்தறி	寺 Buddhist temple புத்த கோவில்	宇 eaves, roof, house, heaven ஈவ்ஸ்	巨 gigantic, big, large, great பிரம்மாண்டமான
震 quake, shake, tremble, quiver, shiver குலுக்கல்	希 hope, beg, request, pray, beseech, Greece நம்பிக்கை	触 contact, touch, feel, hit, proclaim, announce தொடர்பு	依 reliant, depend on, consequently, therefore, due to நம்பகமான
籍 enroll, domiciliary register, membership பதிவு	汚 dirty, pollute, disgrace, rape, defile அழுக்கு	枚 sheet of..., counter for flat thin objects or sheets தாள்	複 duplicate, double, compound, multiple நகல்
郵 mail, stagecoach stop அஞ்சல்	仲 go-between, relationship உறவு	栄 flourish, prosperity, honor, glory, splendor செழித்து வளரும்	札 tag, paper money, counter for bonds, placard, bid குறிச்சொல்
板 plank, board, plate, stage பிளாங்	骨 skeleton, bone, remains, frame எலும்புக்கூடு	傾 lean, incline, tilt, trend, wane, sink, ruin, bias ஒல்லியான	届 deliver, reach, arrive, report, notify, forward வழங்க

Kanji	Meaning	Tamil
巻 (N2)	scroll, volume, book, part, roll up	உருள்
燃 (N2)	burn, blaze, glow	எரிக்க
跡 (N2)	tracks, mark, print, impression	தடங்கள்
包 (N2)	wrap, pack up, cover, conceal	மடக்கு
駐 (N2)	stop-over, reside in, resident	குடியிருப்பாளர்
弱 (N2)	weak, frail	பலவீனமான
紹 (N2)	introduce, inherit, help	அறிமுகப்படுத்துங்கள்
雇 (N2)	employ, hire	வேலை
替 (N2)	exchange, spare, substitute, per-	பரிமாற்றம்
預 (N2)	deposit, custody, leave with, entrust to	வைப்பு
焼 (N2)	bake, burning	சுட்டுக்கொள்ள
簡 (N2)	simplicity, brevity	எளிமை
章 (N2)	badge, chapter, composition, poem, design	பேஜ்
臓 (N2)	entrails, viscera, bowels	குடல்கள்
律 (N2)	rhythm, law, regulation, gauge, control	தாளம்
贈 (N2)	presents, send, give to, award to, confer on	பரிசுகளை
照 (N2)	illuminate, shine, compare, bashful	ஒளிரும்
薄 (N2)	dilute, thin, weak (tea)	நீர்த்த
群 (N2)	flock, group, crowd, herd, swarm, cluster	மந்தை
奥 (N2)	heart, interior	இதயம்

詰 N2	双 N2	刺 N2	純 N2
packed, close, pressed, reprove, rebuke, blame	pair, set, comparison, counter for pairs	thorn, pierce, stab, prick, sting, calling card	genuine, purity, innocence, net (profit)
நிரம்பியுள்ளது	ஜோடி	முள்	நேர்மையான
翌 N2	快 N2	片 N2	敬 N2
the following, next	cheerful, pleasant, agreeable, comfortable	one-sided, leaf, sheet	awe, respect, honor, revere
அடுத்தது	மகிழ்ச்சியான	இலை	பிரமிப்பு
悩 N2	泉 N2	皮 N2	漁 N2
trouble, worry, in pain, distress, illness	spring, fountain	pelt, skin, hide, leather	fishing, fishery
சிக்கல்	வசந்த	pelt	மீன்பிடித்தல்
荒 N2	貯 N2	硬 N2	埋 N2
laid waste, rough, rude, wild	savings, store, lay in, keep, wear mustache	stiff, hard	bury, be filled up, embedded
காட்டு	சேமிப்பு	கடினமான	அடக்கம்
柱 N2	祭 N2	袋 N2	筆 N2
pillar, post, cylinder, support	ritual, offer prayers, celebrate, deify	sack, bag, pouch	writing brush, writing, painting brush, handwriting
தூண்	சடங்கு	கோணி	எழுதுதல்

N2	N2	N2	N2
訓	浴	童	宝
instruction, Japanese character reading	bathe, be favored with, bask in	juvenile, child	treasure, wealth, valuables
அறிவுறுத்தல்	குளிக்கவும்	இளம்	புதையல்

N2	N2	N2	N2
封	胸	砂	塩
seal, closing	bosom, breast, chest, heart, feelings	sand	salt
முத்திரை	மார்பகம்	மணல்	உப்பு

N2	N2	N2	N2
賢	腕	兆	床
intelligent, wise, wisdom, cleverness	arm, ability, talent	portent, 10**12, trillion, sign, omen, symptoms	bed, floor, padding, tatami
புத்திசாலி	கை	அடையாள	படுக்கை

N2	N2	N2	N2
毛	緑	尊	祝
fur, hair, feather, down	green	revered, valuable, precious, noble, exalted	celebrate, congratulate
ஃபர்	பச்சை	மதிக்கப்படுபவர்	கொண்டாடுங்கள்

N2	N2	N2	N2
柔	殿	濃	液
tender, weakness, gentleness, softness	Mr., hall, mansion, palace, temple, lord	concentrated, thick, dark, undiluted	fluid, liquid, juice, sap, secretion
ஒப்பந்தம்	அரண்மனை	குவிந்துள்ளது	திரவம்

衣 N2	肩 N2	零 N2	幼 N2
garment, clothes, dressing	shoulder	zero, spill, overflow, nothing, cipher	infancy, childhood
ஆடை	தோள்பட்டை	பூஜ்யம்	குழந்தை பருவத்தில்
荷 N2	泊 N2	黄 N2	甘 N2
baggage, shoulder-pole load	overnight, put up at, ride at anchor, 3-day stay	yellow	sweet, coax, pamper, be content, sugary
சாமான்கள்	ஒரே இரவில்	மஞ்சள்	இனிப்பு
臣 N2	浅 N2	掃 N2	雲 N2
retainer, subject	shallow, superficial, frivolous, wretched, shameful	sweep, brush	cloud
தக்கவைப்பவர்	மேலோட்டமான	ஸ்வீப்	மேகம்
掘 N2	捨 N2	軟 N2	沈 N2
dig, delve, excavate	discard, throw away, abandon, resign, reject	soft	sink, be submerged, subside, be depressed, aloes
தோண்டி	நிராகரி	மென்மையான	மூழ்கும்
凍 N2	乳 N2	恋 N2	紅 N2
frozen, congeal, refrigerate	milk, breasts	romance, in love, yearn for, miss, darling	crimson, deep red
உறைந்த	பால்	காதல்	கிரிம்சன்

N2 郊	N2 腰	N2 炭	N2 踊
outskirts, suburbs, rural area	loins, hips, waist, low wainscoting	charcoal, coal	jump, dance, leap, skip
புறநகர்ப் பகுதிகள்	இடுப்பு	கரி	குதி

N2 冊	N2 勇	N2 械	N2 菜
tome, counter for books, volume	courage, cheer up, be in high spirits, bravery	contraption, fetter, machine, instrument	vegetable, side dish, greens
எனக்கு	தைரியம்	முரண்பாடு	காய்கறி

N2 珍	N2 卵	N2 湖	N2 喫
rare, curious, strange	egg, ovum, spawn, roe	lake	consume, eat, drink, smoke, receive (a blow)
அரிதானது	முட்டை	ஏரி	நுகரும்

N2 干	N2 虫	N2 刷	N2 湯
dry, parch	insect, bug, temper	printing, print	hot water, bath, hot spring
உலர்ந்த	பூச்சி	அச்சிடுதல்	குளியல்

N2 溶	N2 鉱	N2 涙	N2 匹
melt, dissolve, thaw	mineral, ore	tears, sympathy	equal, head, counter for small animals
உருக	தாது	அனுதாபம்	சமம்

N2	N2	N2	N2
孫	**鋭**	**枝**	**塗**
grandchild, descendants	pointed, sharpness, edge, weapon, sharp, violent	bough, branch, twig, limb	paint, plaster, daub, smear, coating
பேரக்குழந்தை	சுட்டிக்காட்டினார்	bough	பெயிண்ட்
軒	**毒**	**叫**	**拝**
flats, counter for houses, eaves	poison, virus, venom, germ, harm, injury, spite	shout, exclaim, yell	worship, adore, pray to
குடியிருப்புகள்	விஷம்	கூச்சலிடுங்கள்	வழிபாடு
氷	**乾**	**棒**	**祈**
icicle, ice, hail, freeze, congeal	drought, dry, dessicate, drink up, heaven, emperor	rod, stick, cane, pole, club, line	pray, wish
பனிக்கட்டி	வறட்சி	தடி	பிரார்த்தனை
拾	**粉**	**糸**	**綿**
pick up, gather, find, go on foot, ten	flour, powder, dust	thread	cotton
சேகரிக்க	மாவு	நூல்	பருத்தி
汗	**銅**	**湿**	**瓶**
sweat, perspire	copper	damp, wet, moist	flower pot, bottle, vial, jar, jug, vat, urn
வியர்வை	தாமிரம்	ஈரமான	பாட்டில்

N2	N2	N2	N2
咲	召	缶	隻
blossom, bloom	seduce, call, send for, wear, put on, ride in	tin can, container	vessels, counter for ships, fish, birds, arrows
மலரும்	மயக்கு	கொள்கலன்	நாளங்கள்

N2	N2	N2	N2
脂	蒸	肌	耕
fat, grease, tallow, lard, rosin, gum, tar	steam, heat, sultry, foment, get musty	texture, skin, body, grain	till, plow, cultivate
கொழுப்பு	நீராவி	அமைப்பு	வரை

N2	N2	N2	N2
鈍	泥	隅	灯
dull, slow, foolish, blunt	mud, mire, adhere to, be attached to	corner, nook	lamp, a light, light, counter for lights
மந்தமான	சேறு	மூலையில்	விளக்கு

N2	N2	N2	N2
辛	磨	麦	姓
spicy, bitter, hot, acrid	grind, polish, scour, improve, brush (teeth)	barley, wheat	surname
காரமான	அரைக்கவும்	பார்லி	குடும்ப பெயர்

N2	N2	N2	N2
筒	鼻	粒	詞
cylinder, pipe, tube, gun barrel, sleeve	nose, snout	grains, drop, counter for tiny particles	part of speech, words, poetry
சிலிண்டர்	மூக்கு	தானியங்கள்	கவிதை

N2	N2	N2	N2
胃	**畳**	**机**	**膚**
stomach, paunch, crop, craw	tatami mat, counter for tatami mats, fold	desk, table	skin, body, grain, texture, disposition
வயிறு	மடி	மேசை	தோல்
濯	**塔**	**沸**	**灰**
laundry, wash, pour on, rinse	pagoda, tower, steeple	seethe, boil, ferment, uproar, breed	ashes, puckery juice, cremate
சலவை	பகோடா	சீத்தே	சாம்பல்
菓	**帽**	**枯**	**涼**
candy, cakes, fruit	cap, headgear	wither, die, dry up, be seasoned	refreshing, nice and cool
மிட்டாய்	தொப்பி	கவிழ்ந்துவிடும்	புத்துணர்ச்சி
舟	**貝**	**符**	**憎**
boat, ship	shellfish	token, sign, mark, tally, charm	hate, detest
படகு	மட்டி	டோக்கன்	வெறுப்பு
皿	**肯**	**燥**	**畜**
dish, a helping, plate	agreement, consent, comply with	parch, dry up	livestock, domestic fowl and animals
சிறு தட்டு	ஒப்பந்தம்	parch	கால்நடைகள்

挟 N2	曇 N2	滴 N2	伺 N2
pinch, between	cloudy weather, cloud up	drip, drop	pay respects, visit, ask, inquire, question, implore
கிள்ளுதல்	மேகமூட்டம்	சொட்டு மருந்து	வருகை
氏 N2	統 N2	保 N2	第 N2
family name, surname, clan	overall, relationship, ruling, governing	protect, guarantee, keep, preserve, sustain, support	No., residence
குடும்ப பெயர்	ஒட்டுமொத்த	பாதுகாக்க	குடியிருப்பு
結 N2	派 N2	案 N2	策 N2
tie, bind, contract, join, organize, do up hair	faction, group, party, clique, sect, school	plan, suggestion, draft, ponder, fear, proposition	scheme, plan, policy, step, means
கட்டு	பிரிவு	திட்டம்	திட்டம்
基 N2	価 N2	提 N2	挙 N2
fundamentals, radical (chem), counter for machines	value, price	propose, take along, carry in hand	raise, plan, project, behavior, actions
அடிப்படைகள்	மதிப்பு	முன்மொழியுங்கள்	உயர்த்த
応 N2	企 N2	検 N2	沢 N2
apply, answer, yes, OK, reply, accept	undertake, scheme, design, attempt, plan	examination, investigate	swamp
விண்ணப்பிக்கவும்	மேற்கொள்ளுங்கள்	தேர்வு	சதுப்பு நிலம்

裁 N1	証 N1	援 N1	施 N1
tailor, judge, decision, cut out (pattern)	evidence, proof, certificate	abet, help, save	alms, apply bandages, administer first-aid
தையல்காரர்	ஆதாரம்	abet	பிச்சை
井 N1	護 N1	展 N1	態 N1
well, well crib, town, community	safeguard, protect	unfold, expand	attitude, condition, figure, appearance
நன்றாக	பாதுகாத்தல்	திறக்க	அணுகுமுறை
鮮 N1	視 N1	条 N1	幹 N1
fresh, vivid, clear, brilliant, Korea	inspection, regard as, see, look at	article, clause, item, stripe, streak	tree trunk
புதியது	ஆய்வு	கட்டுரை	மரத்தின் தண்டு
独 N1	宮 N1	率 N1	衛 N1
single, alone, spontaneously, Germany	Shinto shrine, constellations, palace, princess	ratio, rate, proportion, %, coefficient, factor	defense, protection
ஒற்றை	இளவரசி	விகிதம்	பாதுகாப்பு
張 N1	監 N1	環 N1	審 N1
lengthen, counter for bows & stringed instruments	oversee, official, govt office, rule, administer	ring, circle, link, wheel	hearing, judge, trial
நீளம்	மேற்பார்வை	சக்கரம்	கேட்டல்

義 N1	訴 N1	株 N1	姿 N1
righteousness, justice, morality, honor, loyalty	accusation, sue, complain of pain, appeal to	stocks, stump, shares, stock	figure, form, shape
நீதி	குற்றச்சாட்டு	பங்குகள்	எண்ணிக்கை
閣 N1	衆 N1	評 N1	影 N1
tower, tall building, palace	masses, great numbers, multitude, populace	evaluate, criticism, comment	shadow, silhouette, phantom
கோபுரம்	வெகுஜன	மதிப்பீடு	நிழல்
松 N1	撃 N1	佐 N1	核 N1
pine tree	beat, attack, defeat, conquer	assistant, help	nucleus, core, kernel
பைன் மரம்	அடி	உதவியாளர்	கரு
整 N1	融 N1	製 N1	票 N1
organize, arranging, tune, tone, meter, key (music)	dissolve, melt	made in..., manufacture	ballot, label, ticket, sign
ஒழுங்கமைக்க	கரை	உற்பத்தி	வாக்குச்சீட்டு
渉 N1	響 N1	推 N1	請 N1
ford, ferry, port	echo, also N5116, sound, resound, ring, vibrate	conjecture, infer, guess, suppose, support	solicit, invite, ask
ஃபோர்ட்	எதிரொலி	அனுமானம்	வேண்டுகோள்

器 N1	士 N1	討 N1	攻 N1
utensil, vessel, receptacle, implement, instrument	gentleman, samurai	chastise, attack, defeat, destroy, conquer	aggression, attack
பாத்திரங்கள்	நற்பண்புகள் கொண்டவர்	தண்டனை	ஆக்கிரமிப்பு

崎 N1	督 N1	授 N1	催 N1
promontory, cape, spit	coach, command, urge, lead, supervise	impart, instruct, grant, confer	sponsor, hold (a meeting), give (a dinner)
விளம்பர	பயிற்சியாளர்	வழங்குங்கள்	ஸ்பான்சர்

及 N1	憲 N1	摘 N1	系 N1
reach out, exert, exercise, cause	constitution, law	pinch, pick, pluck, trim, clip, summarize	lineage, system
முயற்சி	அரசியலமைப்பு	கிள்ளுதல்	பரம்பரை

批 N1	郎 N1	健 N1	盟 N1
criticism, strike	son, counter for sons	healthy, health, strength, persistence	alliance, oath
திறனாய்வு	மகன்	ஆரோக்கியமான	கூட்டணி

従 N1	修 N1	隊 N1	織 N1
accompany, obey, submit to, comply, follow	discipline, conduct oneself well, study, master	regiment, party, company, squad	weave, fabric
உடன்	ஒழுக்கம்	ரெஜிமென்ட்	நெசவு

N1	N1	N1	N1
拡	**故**	**振**	**弁**
broaden, extend, expand, enlarge	happenstance, especially	shake, wave, wag, swing	valve, petal, braid, speech, dialect, discrimination
அகலப்படுத்து	நிகழ்வு	குலுக்கல்	அடைப்பான்
就	**異**	**献**	**厳**
concerning, settle, take position, depart	uncommon, queerness, strangeness, wonderful	offering, counter for drinks, present, offer	stern, strictness, severity, rigidity
பற்றி	அசாதாரணமானது	பிரசாதம்	கடுமையான
維	**浜**	**遺**	**塁**
fiber, tie, rope	seacoast, beach, seashore	bequeath, leave behind, reserve	bases, fort, rampart, walls, base(ball)
ஃபைபர்	கடலோர	bequeath	தளங்கள்
邦	**素**	**遣**	**抗**
home country, country, Japan	elementary, principle, naked, uncovered	despatch, send, give, donate, do, undertake	confront, resist, defy, oppose
நாடு	தொடக்க	அனுப்புதல்	எதிர்கொள்ள
模	**雄**	**益**	**緊**
imitation, copy, mock	masculine, male, hero, leader, superiority	benefit, gain, profit, advantage	tense, solid, hard, reliable, tight
சாயல்	ஆண்பால்	நன்மை	பதற்றமான

標 N1 signpost, seal, mark, stamp, imprint சைன் போஸ்ட்	**宣** N1 proclaim, say, announce அறிவிக்க	**昭** N1 shining, bright பிரகாசிக்கிறது	**廃** N1 abolish, obsolete, cessation, discarding, abandon ஒழித்தல்
伊 N1 Italy, that one இத்தாலி	**江** N1 creek, inlet, bay க்ரீக்	**僚** N1 colleague, official, companion சக	**吉** N1 good luck, joy, congratulations வாழ்த்துக்கள்
皇 N1 emperor பேரரசர்	**臨** N1 look to, face, meet, confront, attend, call on எதிர்கொள்ள	**踏** N1 step, trample, carry through, appraise படி	**壊** N1 demolition, break, destroy இடிப்பு
債 N1 bond, loan, debt பத்திரம்	**興** N1 entertain, revive, retrieve, interest, pleasure பொழுதுபோக்கு	**源** N1 source, origin மூல	**儀** N1 ceremony, rule, affair, case, a matter விழா
創 N1 genesis, wound, injury, hurt, start, originate தோற்றம்	**障** N1 hinder, hurt, harm தடை	**継** N1 inherit, succeed, patch, graft (tree) மரபுரிமையாக	**筋** N1 muscle, sinew, tendon, fiber, plot, plan, descent தசை

闘 N1 fight, war சண்டை	**葬** N1 interment, bury, shelve குறுக்கீடு	**避** N1 evade, avoid, avert, ward off, shirk, shun தவிர்க்கவும்	**司** N1 director, official, govt office, rule, administer இயக்குனர்
康 N1 ease, peace எளிதாக	**善** N1 virtuous, good, goodness நல்லொழுக்கமுள்ள	**逮** N1 apprehend, chase கைது	**迫** N1 urge, force, imminent, spur on தூண்டுதல்
惑 N1 beguile, delusion, perplexity மோசடி	**崩** N1 crumble, die, demolish, level நொறுக்கு	**紀** N1 chronicle, account, narrative, history, annals நாளாகமம்	**聴** N1 listen, headstrong, naughty, careful inquiry கேளுங்கள்
脱 N1 undress, removing, escape from, get rid of ஆடைகளை	**級** N1 class, rank, grade வர்க்கம்	**博** N1 Dr., command, esteem, win acclaim, Ph.D., மரியாதை	**締** N1 tighten, tie, shut, lock, fasten இறுக்கு
救 N1 salvation, save, help, rescue, reclaim இரட்சிப்பு	**執** N1 tenacious, take hold, grasp, take to heart உறுதியான	**房** N1 tassel, tuft, fringe, bunch, lock (hair) விளிம்பு	**撤** N1 remove, withdraw, disarm, dismantle, reject, exclude அகற்று

N1	N1	N1	N1
削 plane, sharpen, whittle, pare விமானம்	**密** secrecy, density (pop), minuteness, carefulness ரகசியம்	**措** set aside, give up, suspend, discontinue, lay aside இடைநீக்கம்	**志** intention, plan, resolve, aspire, motive, hopes நோக்கம்
載 ride, board, get on, place, spread, 10**44 சவாரி	**陣** camp, battle array, ranks, position முகாம்	**我** ego, I, selfish, our, oneself தன்னை	**為** do, change, make, benefit நன்மை
抑 repress, well, now, in the first place, push அடக்கு	**幕** curtain, bunting, act of play திரை	**染** dye, color, paint, stain, print சாயம்	**奈** Nara, what? என்ன?
傷 wound, hurt, injure, impair, pain, injury, cut காயம்	**択** choose, select, elect, prefer தேர்வு செய்யவும்	**秀** excel, excellence, beauty, surpass எக்செல்	**徴** indications, sign, omen, symptom, collect, seek அறிகுறிகள்
弾 bullet, twang, flip, snap புல்லட்	**償** reparation, make up for, recompense, redeem இழப்பீடு	**功** achievement, merits, success, honor, credit சாதனை	**拠** foothold, based on, follow, therefore கால்

N1	N1	N1	N1
秘 secret, conceal ரகசியம்	**拒** repel, refuse, reject, decline விரட்ட	**刑** punish, penalty, sentence, punishment தண்டி	**塚** hillock, mound மலை
致 doth, do, send, forward, cause, exert, incur, engage doth	**繰** winding, reel, spin, turn (pages), look up, refer to முறுக்கு	**尾** tail, end, counter for fish, lower slope of mountain வால்	**描** sketch, compose, write, draw, paint ஸ்கெட்ச்
鈴 small bell, buzzer பஸர்	**盤** tray, shallow bowl, platter, tub, board தட்டு	**項** paragraph, nape of neck, clause, item பத்தி	**喪** miss, mourning துக்கம்
伴 consort, accompany, bring with, companion மனைவி	**養** foster, bring up, rear, develop, nurture வளர்ப்பு	**懸** suspend, hang, 10%, install, depend, consult இடைநீக்கம்	**街** boulevard, street, town பவுல்வர்டு
契 pledge, promise, vow உறுதிமொழி	**掲** put up (a notice), put up, hoist, display காட்சி	**躍** leap, dance, skip பாய்ச்சல்	**棄** abandon, throw away, discard, resign, reject கைவிடு

N1	N1	N1	N1
邸	縮	還	属
residence, mansion	shrink, contract, shrivel, wrinkle, reduce	send back, return	belong, genus, subordinate official, affiliated
குடியிருப்பு	சுருங்க	திரும்ப	சொந்தமானது
慮	枠	恵	露
prudence, thought, concern, consider, deliberate	frame, framework, spindle, spool	favor, blessing, grace, kindness	dew, tears, expose, Russia
வேண்டுமென்றே	சட்டகம்	தயவு	பனி
節	需	射	購
, clause, stanza, honor, joint, knuckle, knob, knot	demand, request, need	shoot, shine into, onto, archery	subscription, buy
முடிச்சு	தேவை	சுடு	சந்தா
揮	充	貢	鹿
brandish, wave, wag, swing, shake	allot, fill	tribute, support, finance	deer
பிராந்தி	ஒதுக்கீடு	அஞ்சலி	மான்
却	端	賃	獲
instead, on the contrary, rather	edge, origin, end, point, border, verge, cape	fare, fee, hire, rent, wages, charge	seize, get, find, earn, acquire, can, may, able to
அதற்கு பதிலாக	விளிம்பு	கட்டணம்	பறிமுதல்

郡
county, district

கவுண்டி

併
join, get together, unite, collective

சேர

徹
penetrate, clear, pierce, strike home

ஊடுருவி

貴
precious, value, prize, esteem, honor

விலைமதிப்பற்றது

衝
collide, brunt, highway, opposition (astronomy)

மோதுக

焦
char, hurry, impatient, irritate, burn, scorch

கரி

奪
rob, take by force, snatch away, dispossess, plunder

கொள்ளை

災
disaster, calamity, woe, curse, evil

பேரழிவு

浦
bay, creek, inlet, gulf, beach, seacoast

விரிகுடா

析
chop, divide, tear, analyze

நறுக்கு

讓
defer, turnover, transfer, convey

ஒத்திவை

称
appellation, praise, admire, name, title, fame

முறையீடு

納
settlement, obtain, reap, pay, supply, store

தீர்வு

樹
timber trees, wood

மரம்

挑
challenge, contend for, make love to

சவால்

誘
entice, lead, tempt, invite, ask, call for

கவர்ந்திழுக்க

紛
distract, be mistaken for, go astray, divert

திசை திருப்ப

至
climax, arrive, proceed, reach, attain, result in

க்ளைமாக்ஸ்

宗
religion, sect, denomination, main point, origin

மதம்

促
stimulate, urge, press, demand, incite

தூண்டுகிறது

慎 N1	控 N1	智 N1	握 N1
humility, be careful, discrete, prudent	withdraw, draw in, hold back, refrain from	wisdom, intellect, reason	grip, hold, mould sushi, bribe
பணிவு	திரும்பப் பெறுங்கள்	ஞானம்	பிடியில்
宙 N1	俊 N1	銭 N1	渋 N1
mid-air, air, space, sky, memorization	sagacious, genius, excellence	coin, .01 yen, money	astringent, hesitate, reluctant, have diarrhea
மனப்பாடம்	sagacious	நாணயம்	மூச்சுத்திணறல்
銃 N1	操 N1	携 N1	診 N1
gun, arms	maneuver, manipulate, operate, steer, chastity	portable, carry (in hand), armed with, bring along	checkup, seeing, diagnose, examine
ஆயுதங்கள்	சூழ்ச்சி	சிறிய	சோதனை
託 N1	撮 N1	誕 N1	侵 N1
consign, requesting, entrusting with, pretend, hint	snapshot, take pictures	nativity, be born, declension, lie, be arbitrary	encroach, invade, raid, trespass, violate
சரக்கு	ஸ்னாப்ஷாட்	நேட்டிவிட்டி	மீறு
括 N1	謝 N1	駆 N1	透 N1
fasten, tie up, arrest, constrict	apologize, thank, refuse	drive, run, gallop, advance, inspire, impel	transparent, permeate, filter, penetrate
கட்டு	மன்னிப்பு கேளுங்கள்	தூண்டுதல்	ஒளி புகும்

津 **N1**	壁 **N1**	稲 **N1**	仮 **N1**
haven, port, harbor, ferry	wall, lining (stomach), fence	rice plant	sham, temporary, interim, assumed (name), informal
புகலிடம்	வேலி	அரிசி ஆலை	ஷாம்
裂 **N1**	敏 **N1**	是 **N1**	排 **N1**
split, rend, tear	cleverness, agile, alert	just so, this, right, justice	repudiate, exclude, expel, reject
பிளவு	புத்திசாலித்தனம்	நீதி	நிராகரிக்க
裕 **N1**	堅 **N1**	訳 **N1**	芝 **N1**
abundant, rich, fertile	strict, hard, solid, tough, tight, reliable	translate, reason, circumstance, case	turf, lawn
ஏராளமாக	கண்டிப்பான	மொழிபெயர்	தரை
綱 **N1**	典 **N1**	賀 **N1**	扱 **N1**
hawser, class (genus), rope, cord, cable	code, ceremony, law, rule	congratulations, joy	handle, entertain, thresh, strip
hawser	குறியீடு	வாழ்த்துக்கள்	கைப்பிடி
顧 **N1**	弘 **N1**	看 **N1**	訟 **N1**
look back, review, examine oneself, turn around	vast, broad, wide	watch over, see	sue, accuse
விமர்சனம்	பரந்த	பார்க்க	குற்றம்

N1	N1	N1	N1
戒	祉	誉	歓
commandment	welfare, happiness	reputation, praise, honor, glory	delight, joy
கட்டளை	நலன்புரி	நற்பெயர்	மகிழ்ச்சி

N1	N1	N1	N1
奏	勧	騒	閥
play music, speak to a ruler, complete	persuade, recommend, advise, encourage, offer	boisterous, make noise, clamor, disturb, excite	clique, lineage, pedigree, faction, clan
முழுமை	சம்மதிக்க	கொந்தளிப்பான	குழு

N1	N1	N1	N1
甲	縄	郷	揺
armor, high (voice), A grade, first class, former	straw rope, cord	home town, village, native place, district	swing, shake, sway, rock, tremble, vibrate
கவசம்	தண்டு	கிராமம்	ஸ்விங்

N1	N1	N1	N1
免	既	薦	隣
excuse, dismissal	previously, already, long ago	recommend, mat, advise, encourage, offer	neighboring
சாக்குப்போக்கு	முன்பு	பரிந்துரை	அண்டை அயலார்

N1	N1	N1	N1
華	範	隠	徳
splendor, flower, petal, shine, luster, ostentatious	pattern, example, model	conceal, hide, cover	benevolence, virtue, goodness, commanding respect
அற்புதம்	முறை	மறை	நன்மை

哲 N1 philosophy, clear தத்துவம்	**杉** N1 cedar, cryptomeria சிடார்	**釈** N1 explanation விளக்கம்	**己** N1 self, snake, serpent பாம்பு
妥 N1 gentle, peace, depravity மென்மையான	**威** N1 intimidate, dignity, majesty, menace, threaten மிரட்டுங்கள்	**豪** N1 overpowering, great, powerful, excelling, Australia அதிக சக்தி	**熊** N1 bear தாங்க
滞 N1 stagnate, be delayed, overdue, arrears தேக்கம்	**微** N1 delicate, minuteness, insignificance மென்மையான	**隆** N1 hump, high, noble, prosperity கூம்பு	**症** N1 symptoms, illness அறிகுறிகள்
暫 N1 temporarily, a while, moment, long time தற்காலிகமாக	**忠** N1 loyalty, fidelity, faithfulness விசுவாசம்	**倉** N1 godown, warehouse, storehouse, cellar, treasury கிடங்கு	**彦** N1 lad, boy (ancient) பையன்
肝 N1 liver, pluck, nerve, chutzpah கல்லீரல்	**喚** N1 yell, cry, scream கத்தவும்	**沿** N1 run alongside, follow along, run along, lie along பின்தொடரவும்	**妙** N1 exquisite, strange, queer, mystery, miracle நேர்த்தியான

N1	N1	N1	N1
唱 chant, recite, call upon, yell மந்திரம்	阿 Africa, flatter, fawn upon, corner, nook, recess மூலையில்	索 cord, rope தண்டு	誠 sincerity, admonish, warn, prohibit, truth நேர்மை
襲 attack, advance on, succeed to, pile, heap தாக்குதல்	懇 sociable, kind, courteous, hospitable, cordial நேசமான	俳 haiku, actor நடிகர்	柄 design, pattern, build, nature, handle, crank வடிவமைப்பு
驚 wonder, be surprised, frightened, amazed ஆச்சரியம்	麻 hemp, flax சணல்	李 plum பிளம்	浩 wide expanse, abundance, vigorous வீரியம்
剤 dose, medicine, drug டோஸ்	瀬 rapids, current, torrent, shallows, shoal ரேபிட்கள்	趣 gist, proceed to, tend, become சுருக்கம்	陥 collapse, fall into, cave in, fall (castle) சரிவு
斎 purification, Buddhist food, room, worship, avoid சுத்திகரிப்பு	貫 pierce, 8 1, 3lbs, penetrate, brace துளை	仙 hermit, wizard, cent துறவி	慰 consolation, amusement, seduce, cheer, console ஆறுதல்

序 N1 preface, beginning, order, precedence, occasion முன்னுரை	**兼** N1 concurrently, and ஒரே நேரத்தில்	**聖** N1 holy, saint, sage, master, priest பரிசுத்த	**旨** N1 delicious, relish, show a liking for, purport, will சுவையானது
即 N1 instant, namely, as is, conform, agree, adapt உடனடி	**柳** N1 willow வில்லோ	**舎** N1 cottage, inn, hut, house, mansion குடிசை	**偽** N1 falsehood, lie, deceive, pretend, counterfeit பொய்
較 N1 contrast, compare மாறாக	**覇** N1 hegemony, supremacy, leadership, champion மேலாதிக்கம்	**詳** N1 detailed, full, minute, accurate, well-informed விரிவானது	**抵** N1 resist, reach, touch எதிர்க்க
脅 N1 threaten, coerce அச்சுறுத்தல்	**茂** N1 overgrown, grow thick, be luxuriant மிகைப்படுத்தப்பட்ட	**犠** N1 sacrifice தியாகம்	**旗** N1 national flag, banner, standard தரநிலை
距 N1 long-distance நீண்ட தூரம்	**雅** N1 gracious, elegant, graceful, refined கருணை	**飾** N1 decorate, ornament, adorn, embellish அலங்கரிக்க	**網** N1 netting, network வலையமைப்பு

竜 (N1)	詩 (N1)	繁 (N1)	翼 (N1)
dragon, imperial	poem, poetry	luxuriant, thick, overgrown, frequency, complexity	wing, plane, flank
டிராகன்	கவிதை	ஆடம்பரமான	சாரி
潟 (N1)	敵 (N1)	魅 (N1)	嫌 (N1)
lagoon	enemy, foe, opponent	fascination, charm, bewitch	dislike, detest, hate
குளம்	எதிரி	மோகம்	வெறுப்பு
斉 (N1)	敷 (N1)	擁 (N1)	圏 (N1)
adjusted, alike, equal, similar variety of	spread, pave, sit, promulgate	hug, embrace, possess, protect, lead	sphere, circle, radius, range
சரிசெய்யப்பட்ட	பரவுதல்	கட்டிப்பிடி	கோளம்
酸 (N1)	罰 (N1)	滅 (N1)	礎 (N1)
acid, bitterness, sour, tart	penalty, punishment	destroy, ruin, overthrow, perish	cornerstone, foundation stone
அமிலம்	தண்டம்	அழிக்க	மூலையில்
腐 (N1)	潮 (N1)	梅 (N1)	尽 (N1)
rot, decay, sour	tide, salt water, opportunity	plum	exhaust, use up, run out of, befriend, serve
அழுகல்	அலை	பிளம்	வெளியேற்ற

僕 (N1) me, I (male) என்னை	**桜** (N1) cherry செர்ரி	**滑** (N1) slippery, slide, slip, flunk வழுக்கும்	**孤** (N1) orphan, alone அனாதை
炎 (N1) inflammation, flame, blaze வீக்கம்	**賠** (N1) compensation, indemnify இழப்பீடு	**句** (N1) phrase, clause, sentence, passage, paragraph சொற்றொடர்	**鋼** (N1) steel எஃகு
頑 (N1) stubborn, foolish, firmly பிடிவாதமான	**鎖** (N1) chain, irons, connection சங்கிலி	**彩** (N1) coloring, paint, makeup வண்ணமயமாக்கல்	**摩** (N1) chafe, rub, polish, grind, scrape chafe
励 (N1) encourage, be diligent, inspire ஊக்குவிக்கவும்	**縦** (N1) vertical, length, height, self-indulgent, wayward செங்குத்து	**輝** (N1) radiance, shine, sparkle, gleam, twinkle பிரகாசம்	**蓄** (N1) amass, keeping a concubine, phonograph குவித்தல்
軸 (N1) axis, pivot, stem, stalk, counter for book scrolls அச்சு	**巡** (N1) patrol, go around, circumference ரோந்து	**稼** (N1) earnings, work, earn money வருவாய்	**瞬** (N1) wink, blink, twinkle கண் சிமிட்டும்

砲	噴	誇	祥
cannon, gun	erupt, spout, emit, flush out	boast, be proud, pride, triumphantly	auspicious, happiness, good omen
பீரங்கி	வெடிக்கும்	பெருமை	சுப
牲	秩	帝	宏
animal sacrifice, offering	regularity, salary, order	sovereign, the emperor, god, creator	wide, large
பிரசாதம்	வழக்கமான	இறையாண்மை	பரந்த
唆	阻	泰	賄
tempt, seduce, instigate, promote	thwart, separate from, prevent, obstruct, deter	peaceful, calm, peace, easy, Thailand	bribe, board, supply, finance
தூண்டுதல்	தடுக்க	அமைதியான	கையூட்டு
撲	堀	菊	絞
slap, strike, hit, beat, tell, speak	ditch, moat, canal	chrysanthemum	strangle, constrict, wring
அறைந்து விடு	பள்ளம்	கிரிசான்தமம்	கழுத்தை நெரிக்க
縁	唯	膨	矢
affinity, relation, connection, edge, border	solely, only, merely, simply	swell, get fat, thick	dart, arrow
உறவு	முற்றிலும்	வீக்கம்	டார்ட்

Kanji	English	Tamil
耐 (N1)	-proof, enduring	நீடித்த
塾 (N1)	cram school, private school	தனியார் பள்ளி
漏 (N1)	leak, escape, time	கசிவு
慶 (N1)	jubilation, congratulate, rejoice, be happy	மகிழ்ச்சி
猛 (N1)	fierce, rave, rush, become furious, wildness	கடுமையான
芳 (N1)	perfume, balmy, flavorable, fragrant	வாசனை
懲 (N1)	penal, chastise, punish, discipline	அபராதம்
剣 (N1)	sabre, sword, blade, clock hand	saber
彰 (N1)	patent, clear	காப்புரிமை
棋 (N1)	chess piece, Japanese chess, shogi	ஷோகி
丁 (N1)	street, ward, town	தெரு
恒 (N1)	constancy, always	நிலையான
揚 (N1)	hoist, fry in deep fat	ஏற்றம்
冒 (N1)	risk, face, defy, dare, damage, assume (a name)	ஆபத்து
之 (N1)	of, this	இது
倫 (N1)	ethics, companion	நெறிமுறைகள்
陳 (N1)	exhibit, state, relate, explain	கண்காட்சி
憶 (N1)	recollection, think, remember	நினைவு
梨 (N1)	pear tree	பேரிக்காய் மரம்
仁 (N1)	humanity, virtue, benevolence, charity, man, kernel	மனிதநேயம்

N1	N1	N1	N1
克	**岳**	**概**	**拘**
overcome, kindly, skillfully	point, peak, mountain	outline, condition, approximation, generally	arrest, seize, concerned, adhere to, despite
கடந்து வா	புள்ளி	அவுட்லைன்	கைது
墓	**黙**	**須**	**偏**
grave, tomb	silence, become silent, stop speaking, leave as is	ought, by all means, necessarily	partial, side, left-side radical, inclining, biased
கல்லறை	ம .னம்	கட்டாயம்	பகுதி
霧	**遇**	**諮**	**狭**
atmosphere, fog	interview, treat, entertain, receive, deal with	consult with	cramped, narrow, contract, tight
வளிமண்டலம்	நேர்காணல்	ஆலோசனை	தடைபட்டது
卓	**亀**	**糧**	**簿**
eminent, table, desk, high	tortoise, turtle	provisions, food, bread	register, record book
சிறந்த	ஆமை	விதிகள்	பதிவு
炉	**牧**	**殊**	**殖**
hearth, furnace, kiln, reactor	breed, care for, shepherd, feed, pasture	particularly, especially, exceptionally	augment, increase, multiply, raise
அடுப்பு	இனப்பெருக்கம்	குறிப்பாக	பெருக்குதல்

N1	N1	N1	N1
艦	**輩**	**穴**	**奇**
warship	comrade, fellow, people, companions	hole, aperture, slit, cave, den	strange, strangeness, curiosity
போர்க்கப்பல்	தோழர்	துளை	விசித்திரமானது
N1	N1	N1	N1
慢	**鶴**	**謀**	**暖**
ridicule, laziness	crane, stork	conspire, cheat, impose on, plan, devise, scheme	warmth
ஏளனம்	கிரேன்	சதி	அரவணைப்பு
N1	N1	N1	N1
昌	**拍**	**朗**	**寛**
prosperous, bright, clear	clap, beat (music)	melodious, clear, bright, serene, cheerful	tolerant, leniency, generosity, relax, feel at home
வளமான	கைதட்டல்	மெல்லிசை	சகிப்புத்தன்மை
N1	N1	N1	N1
覆	**胞**	**泣**	**隔**
capsize, cover, shade, mantle, be ruined	placenta, sac, sheath	cry, weep, moan	isolate, alternate, distance, separate, gulf
கேப்சைஸ்	நஞ்சுக்கொடி	கலங்குவது	தனிமைப்படுத்து
N1	N1	N1	N1
浄	**没**	**暇**	**肺**
clean, purify, cleanse, exorcise, Manchu Dynasty	drown, sink, hide, fall into, disappear, die	spare time, rest, leisure, time, leave of absence	lungs
சுத்தமான	மூழ்கி	ஓய்வு	நுரையீரல்

N1	N1	N1	N1
貞	**靖**	**鑑**	**飼**
upright, chastity, constancy, righteousness	peaceful	specimen, take warning from, learn from	domesticate, raise, keep, feed
நிமிர்ந்து	அமைதியான	மாதிரி	வளர்ப்பு
陰	**銘**	**随**	**烈**
shade, yin, negative, sex organs, secret, shadow	inscription, signature (of artisan)	follow, though, notwithstanding	ardent, violent, vehement, furious, severe, extreme
நிழல்	கல்வெட்டு	பின்தொடரவும்	தீவிரமான
尋	**稿**	**丹**	**啓**
inquire, fathom, look for	draft, copy, manuscript, straw	rust-colored, red, red lead, pills	disclose, open, say
விசாரிக்கவும்	வரைவு	மாத்திரைகள்	வெளிப்படுத்து
也	**丘**	**壌**	**漫**
to be (classical)	hill, knoll	lot, earth, soil	cartoon, involuntarily, in spite of oneself
இருக்க வேண்டும்	மலை	மண்	கார்ட்டூன்
玄	**粘**	**悟**	**舗**
mysterious, occultness	sticky, glutinous, greasy, persevere	enlightenment, perceive, discern, realize	shop, store
மர்மமான	ஒட்டும்	அறிவொளி	கடை

妊 (N1) pregnancy கர்ப்பம்	熟 (N1) mellow, ripen, mature, acquire skill மெல்லோ	旭 (N1) rising sun, morning sun உதய சூரியன்	恩 (N1) grace, kindness, goodness, favor, mercy கருணை
騰 (N1) inflation, advancing, going வீக்கம்	往 (N1) journey, chase away, let go, going, travel பயணம்	豆 (N1) beans, pea, midget பீன்ஸ்	遂 (N1) consummate, accomplish, attain, commit (suicide) முழுமையான
狂 (N1) lunatic, insane, crazy, confuse பைத்தியம்	岐 (N1) branch off, fork in road, scene, arena, theater திரையரங்கம்	陛 (N1) highness, steps (of throne) உயர்ந்த தன்மை	緯 (N1) horizontal, woof, left & right, latitude கிடைமட்ட
培 (N1) cultivate, foster பயிரிடவும்	衰 (N1) decline, wane, weaken சரிவு	艇 (N1) rowboat, small boat ரோபோட்	屈 (N1) yield, bend, flinch, submit மகசூல்
径 (N1) diameter, path, method விட்டம்	淡 (N1) thin, faint, pale, fleeting மெல்லிய	抽 (N1) pluck, pull, extract, excel பறிக்க	披 (N1) expose, open அம்பலப்படுத்து

Kanji	Meaning	Tamil
廷 (N1)	courts, imperial court, government office	நீதிமன்றங்கள்
錦 (N1)	brocade, fine dress, honors	ப்ரோக்கேட்
准 (N1)	quasi-, semi-, associate	இணை
暑 (N1)	sultry, hot, summer heat	புத்திசாலித்தனமான
磯 (N1)	seashore, beach	கடற்கரை
奨 (N1)	exhort, urge, encourage	அறிவுறுத்துங்கள்
浸 (N1)	immersed, soak, dip, steep, moisten, wet, dunk	மூழ்கியது
剰 (N1)	surplus, besides	உபரி
胆 (N1)	gall bladder, courage, pluck, nerve	தைரியம்
繊 (N1)	slender, fine, thin kimono	மெல்லிய
駒 (N1)	pony, horse, colt	மட்டக்குதிரை
虚 (N1)	void, emptiness, unpreparedness, crack, fissure	வெற்றிடத்தை
霊 (N1)	spirits, soul	ஆவிகள்
帳 (N1)	notebook, account book, album	நோட்புக்
悔 (N1)	repent, regret	மனந்திரும்புங்கள்
諭 (N1)	rebuke, admonish, charge, warn, persuade	கண்டி
惨 (N1)	wretched, disaster, cruelty, harsh	மோசமான
虐 (N1)	tyrannize, oppress	கொடுங்கோன்மை
翻 (N1)	flip, turn over, wave, flutter, change (mind)	புரட்டு
墜 (N1)	crash, fall (down)	செயலிழப்பு

沼 N1 marsh, lake, bog, swamp, pond சதுப்பு நிலம்	**据** N1 set, lay a foundation, install, equip, squat down நிறுவு	**肥** N1 fertilizer, get fat, fertile, manure, pamper உரம்	**徐** N1 gradually, slowly, deliberately, gently படிப்படியாக
糖 N1 sugar சர்க்கரை	**搭** N1 board, load (a vehicle), ride பலகை	**盾** N1 shield, escutcheon, pretext கவசம்	**脈** N1 vein, pulse, hope நரம்பு
滝 N1 waterfall, rapids, cascade நீர்வீழ்ச்சி	**軌** N1 rut, wheel, track, model, way of doing ரூட்	**俵** N1 bag, bale, sack, counter for bags பை	**妨** N1 disturb, prevent, hamper, obstruct தொந்தரவு
擦 N1 grate, rub, scratch, scrape, chafe, scour தட்டி	**鯨** N1 whale திமிங்கிலம்	**荘** N1 villa, inn, cottage, feudal manor வில்லா	**諾** N1 consent, assent, agreement ஒப்புதல்
雷 N1 thunder, lightening bolt இடி	**漂** N1 drift, float (on liquid) சறுக்கல்	**懐** N1 pocket, feelings, heart, yearn, miss someone பாக்கெட்	**勘** N1 intuition, perception உள்ளுணர்வு

栽 N1 plantation, planting தோட்டம்	**拐** N1 kidnap, falsify கடத்தல்	**駄** N1 burdensome, pack horse, horse load, send by horse சுமை	**添** N1 annexed, accompany, marry, suit, meet இணைக்கப்பட்டது
冠 N1 crown, best, peerless கிரீடம்	**斜** N1 diagonal, slanting, oblique மூலைவிட்ட	**鏡** N1 mirror, speculum, barrel-head கண்ணாடி	**聡** N1 wise, fast learner பாண்டித்தியம்
浪 N1 wandering, waves, billows அலைந்து திரிகிறது	**亜** N1 Asia, rank next, come after, -ous ஆசியா	**覧** N1 perusal, see perusal	**詐** N1 lie, falsehood, deceive, pretend பொய்
壇 N1 podium, stage, rostrum, terrace மேடை	**勲** N1 meritorious deed, merit தகுதி	**魔** N1 witch, demon, evil spirit சூனியக்காரி	**酬** N1 repay, reward, retribution திருப்பிச் செலுத்துங்கள்
紫 N1 purple, violet ஊதா	**曙** N1 dawn, daybreak விடியல்	**紋** N1 family crest, figures புள்ளிவிவரங்கள்	**卸** N1 wholesale மொத்த

奮 N1 stirred up, be invigorated, flourish செழித்து வளரும்	**欄** N1 column, handrail, blank, space நெடுவரிசை	**逸** N1 deviate, idleness, leisure, miss the mark, evade விலகல்	**涯** N1 horizon, shore அடிவானம்
拓 N1 clear (the land), open, break up (land) திறந்த	**眼** N1 eyeball கண் பார்வை	**獄** N1 prison, jail சிறையில்	**尚** N1 esteem, furthermore, still, yet மரியாதை
彫 N1 carve, engrave, chisel செதுக்கும்	**穏** N1 calm, quiet, moderation அமைதியாக	**顕** N1 appear, existing தோன்றும்	**巧** N1 adroit, skilled, ingenuity adroit
矛 N1 halberd, arms, festival float ஹில்பர்ட்	**垣** N1 hedge, fence, wall ஹெட்ஜ்	**欺** N1 deceit, cheat, delude வஞ்சகம்	**萩** N1 bush clover புஷ் க்ளோவர்
粛 N1 solemn, quietly, softly புனிதமான	**栗** N1 chestnut கஷ்கொட்டை	**愚** N1 foolish, folly, absurdity, stupid முட்டாள்	**遭** N1 encounter, meet, party, association, interview என்கவுண்டர்

架 (N1) erect, frame, mount, support, shelf, construct நிமிர்ந்து	**鬼** (N1) ghost, devil பேய்	**庶** (N1) commoner, all, bastard பொதுவானது	**稚** (N1) immature, young முதிர்ச்சியற்ற
滋 (N1) nourishing, more & more, be luxuriant ஊட்டமளிக்கும்	**幻** (N1) phantasm, vision, dream, illusion, apparition phantasm	**煮** (N1) boil, cook சமைக்கவும்	**姫** (N1) princess இளவரசி
誓 (N1) vow, swear, pledge சபதம்	**把** (N1) grasp, faggot, bunch, counter for bundles கிரகித்தல்	**践** (N1) tread, step on, trample, practice, carry through ஜாக்கிரதையாக	**呈** (N1) display, offer, present, send, exhibit காட்சி
疎 (N1) alienate, rough, neglect, shun, sparse அந்நியப்படுத்து	**仰** (N1) face-up, look up, depend, seek, respect, rever மரியாதை	**剛** (N1) sturdy, strength துணிவுமிக்க	**疾** (N1) rapidly விரைவாக
征 (N1) subjugate, attack the rebellious, collect taxes அடிபணியுங்கள்	**砕** (N1) smash, break, crush, familiar, popular நொறுக்கு	**嫁** (N1) marry into, bride மணப்பெண்	**謙** (N1) self-effacing, humble oneself, condescend condescend

后 (N1) empress, queen, after, behind, back, later பின்னர்	**嘆** (N1) sigh, lament, moan, grieve பெருமூச்சு	**菌** (N1) germ, fungus, bacteria கிருமி	**鎌** (N1) sickle, scythe, trick அரிவாள்
巣 (N1) nest, rookery, hive, cobweb, den கூடு	**頻** (N1) repeatedly, recur மீண்டும் மீண்டும்	**琴** (N1) harp, koto வீணை	**班** (N1) squad, corps, unit, group அணி
棚 (N1) shelf, ledge, rack, mount, mantle, trellis அலமாரி	**潔** (N1) undefiled, pure, clean, righteous, gallant வரையறுக்கப்படாதத	**酷** (N1) cruel, severe, atrocious, unjust கொடுமை	**宰** (N1) superintend, manager, rule கண்காணிப்பாளர்
廊 (N1) corridor, hall, tower தாழ்வாரம்	**寂** (N1) loneliness, quietly, mellow, mature தனிமை	**辰** (N1) sign of the dragon, 7-9AM டிராகனின் அடையாளம்	**霞** (N1) be hazy, grow dim, blurred மங்கலான
伏 (N1) prostrated, bend down, bow, cover, lay (pipes) சிரம் பணிந்தது	**碁** (N1) Go போ	**俗** (N1) vulgar, customs, manners, worldliness மோசமான	**漠** (N1) vague, obscure, desert, wide தெளிவற்ற

邪 (N1) wicked, injustice, wrong பொல்லாத	**晶** (N1) sparkle, clear, crystal பிரகாசம்	**墨** (N1) black ink, India ink, ink stick, Mexico கருப்பு மை	**鎮** (N1) tranquilize, ancient peace-preservation centers அமைதி
洞 (N1) den, cave, excavation டென்	**履** (N1) footgear, shoes, boots, put on (the feet footgear	**劣** (N1) inferiority, be inferior to, be worse தாழ்வு மனப்பான்மை	**那** (N1) what? என்ன?
殴 (N1) assault, hit, beat, thrash தாக்குதல்	**娠** (N1) with child, pregnancy கர்ப்பம்	**奉** (N1) observance, offer, present, dedicate அனுசரிப்பு	**憂** (N1) melancholy, grieve, lament, be anxious, sad துக்கம்
朴 (N1) crude, simple, plain, docile கச்சா	**亭** (N1) pavilion, restaurant, mansion, arbor, cottage பெவிலியன்	**淳** (N1) pure தூய்மையானது	**怪** (N1) suspicious, mystery, apparition சந்தேகத்திற்குரியது
鳩 (N1) pigeon, dove புறா	**酔** (N1) drunk, feel sick, poisoned, elated, spellbound குடித்துவிட்டு	**惜** (N1) pity, be sparing of, frugal, stingy, regret பரிதாபம்	**穫** (N1) harvest, reap அறுவடை

佳 N1	潤 N1	悼 N1	乏 N1
excellent, beautiful, good, pleasing, skilled	wet, be watered, profit by, receive benefits	lament, grieve over	destitution, scarce, limited
சிறந்தது	ஈரமான	புலம்பல்	வறுமை
該 N1	赴 N1	桑 N1	桂 N1
above-stated, the said, that specific	proceed, get, become, tend	mulberry	Japanese Judas-tree, cinnamon tree
குறிப்பிட்ட	தொடரவும்	மல்பெரி	இலவங்கப்பட்டை மரம்
髄 N1	虎 N1	盆 N1	晋 N1
marrow, pith	tiger, drunkard	basin, lantern festival, tray	advance
மஜ்ஜை	புலி	பேசின்	முன்கூட்டியே
穂 N1	壮 N1	堤 N1	飢 N1
ear, ear (grain), head, crest (wave)	robust, manhood, prosperity	dike, bank, embankment	hungry, starve
காது	வலுவான	டைக்	பசி
傍 N1	疫 N1	累 N1	痴 N1
bystander, side, besides, while, nearby, 3rd person	epidemic	accumulate, involvement, trouble, tie up	stupid, foolish
பார்வையாளர்	பெருவாரியாக பரவும் தொற்று	குவிதல்	முட்டாள்

搬 N1	晃 N1	癒 N1	寸 N1
conveyor, carry, transport	clear	healing, cure, quench (thirst), wreak	measurement, foot, 10
கன்வேயர்	தெளிவானது	குணப்படுத்துதல்	அளவீட்டு
郭 N1	尿 N1	凶 N1	吐 N1
enclosure, quarters, fortification	urine	villain, evil, bad luck, disaster	spit, vomit, belch, confess, tell (lies)
அடைப்பு	சிறுநீர்	வில்லன்	துப்ப
宴 N1	鷹 N1	賓 N1	虜 N1
banquet, feast, party	hawk	V.I.P., guest	captive, barbarian, low epithet for the enemy
விருந்து	பருந்து	விருந்தினர்	றைப்பிடிக்கப்பட்டவ
陶 N1	鐘 N1	憾 N1	猪 N1
pottery, porcelain	bell, gong, chimes	remorse, regret, be sorry	boar
மட்பாண்டங்கள்	மணி	மனஉளைவு	பன்றி
紘 N1	磁 N1	弥 N1	昆 N1
large	magnet, porcelain	all the more, increasingly	descendants, elder brother, insect
பெரியது	காந்தம்	பெருகிய முறையில்	சந்ததியினர்

粗 N1 coarse, rough, rugged கரடுமுரடான	**訂** N1 revise, correct, decide திருத்தவும்	**芽** N1 bud, sprout, spear, germ மொட்டு	**庄** N1 level நிலை
傘 N1 umbrella குடை	**敦** N1 industry, kindliness தொழில்	**騎** N1 equestrian, riding on horses குதிரையேற்றம்	**寧** N1 rather, preferably மாறாக
循 N1 sequential, fellow தொடர்ச்சியான	**忍** N1 endure, bear, put up with, conceal, secrete தாங்க	**怠** N1 neglect, laziness புறக்கணிப்பு	**如** N1 likeness, like, such as, as if, better, best, equal ஒற்றுமை
寮 N1 dormitory, hostel, villa, tea pavillion தங்குமிடம்	**祐** N1 help உதவி	**鵬** N1 phoenix பீனிக்ஸ்	**鉛** N1 lead வழி நடத்து
珠 N1 pearl, gem, jewel முத்து	**苗** N1 seedling, sapling, shoot நாற்று	**獣** N1 animal, beast விலங்கு	**哀** N1 pathetic, grief, sorrow, pathos, pity, sympathize பரிதாபகரமான

<table>
<tr>
<td>

跳 N1

hop, leap up, spring, jerk, prance, buck, splash

ஹாப்

</td>
<td>

匠 N1

artisan, workman, carpenter

கைவினைஞர்

</td>
<td>

垂 N1

droop, suspend, hang, slouch

துளி

</td>
<td>

蛇 N1

snake, serpent, hard drinker

பாம்பு

</td>
</tr>
<tr>
<td>

澄 N1

lucidity, be clear, clear, clarify, settle, strain

தெளிவு

</td>
<td>

縫 N1

sew, stitch, embroider

தை

</td>
<td>

僧 N1

Buddhist priest, monk

துறவி

</td>
<td>

眺 N1

stare, watch, look at, see, scrutinize

முறைத்துப் பாருங்கள்

</td>
</tr>
<tr>
<td>

亘 N1

span, request

span

</td>
<td>

呉 N1

give, do something for

கொடுங்கள்

</td>
<td>

凡 N1

mediocre

சாதாரணமான

</td>
<td>

憩 N1

recess, rest, relax, repose

இடைவெளி

</td>
</tr>
<tr>
<td>

媛 N1

beautiful woman, princess

இளவரசி

</td>
<td>

溝 N1

gutter, ditch, sewer, drain, 10**32

குழல்

</td>
<td>

恭 N1

respect, reverent

மரியாதை

</td>
<td>

刈 N1

reap, cut, clip, trim, prune

அறுவடை

</td>
</tr>
<tr>
<td>

睡 N1

drowsy, sleep, die

மயக்கம்

</td>
<td>

錯 N1

confused, mix, be in disorder

குழப்பமான

</td>
<td>

伯 N1

chief, count, earl, uncle, Brazil

தலைமை

</td>
<td>

笹 N1

bamboo grass

மூங்கில் புல்

</td>
</tr>
</table>

N1
穀
cereals, grain
தானியங்கள்

N1
陵
mausoleum, imperial tomb
கல்லறை

N1
霧
fog, mist
மூடுபனி, மூடுபனி

N1
魂
soul, spirit
ஆன்மா

N1
弊
abuse, evil, vice, breakage
துஷ்பிரயோகம்

N1
妃
queen, princess
ராணி

N1
舶
liner, ship
லைனர்

N1
餓
starve, hungry, thirst
பட்டினி கிடக்கிறது

N1
窮
hard up, destitute, suffer, perplexed, cornered
ஆதரவற்றவர்கள்

N1
掌
manipulate, rule, administer, conduct, palm of hand
கையாளுங்கள்

N1
麗
lovely, companion
அழகான

N1
綾
design, figured cloth, twill
வடிவமைப்பு

N1
臭
stinking, ill-smelling, suspicious looking
துர்நாற்றம் வீசுகிறது

N1
悦
ecstasy, joy, rapture
பரவசம்

N1
刃
blade, sword, edge
கத்தி

N1
縛
truss, arrest, bind, tie, restrain
டிரஸ்

N1
曆
calendar, almanac
நாட்காட்டி

N1
宜
best regards, good
வாழ்த்துக்கள்

N1
盲
blind, blind man, ignoramus
குருட்டு

N1
粋
chic, style, purity, essence, pith, cream, elite
நடை

N1	N1	N1	N1
辱	毅	轄	猿
embarrass, humiliate, shame	strong	control, wedge	monkey
சங்கடம்	வலுவான	கட்டுப்பாடு	குரங்கு
弦	稔	窒	炊
bowstring, chord, hypotenuse	harvest, ripen	plug up, obstruct	cook, boil
வில்லு	அறுவடை	தடை	சமைக்கவும்
洪	摂	飽	冗
deluge, flood, vast	vicarious, surrogate, act in addition to	sated, tired of, bored, satiate	superfluous, uselessness
பிரளயம்	தீங்கு விளைவிக்கும்	sated	மிதமிஞ்சிய
桃	狩	朱	渦
peach tree	hunt, raid, gather	vermilion, cinnabar, scarlet, red, bloody	whirlpool, eddy, vortex
குழிப்பேரி மரம்	வேட்டை	வெர்மிலியன்	வேர்ல்பூல்
紳	枢	碑	鍛
sire, good belt, gentleman	hinge, pivot, door	tombstone, monument	forge, discipline, train
நற்பண்புகள் கொண்டவர்	கீல்	கல்லறை	மோசடி

刀 N1	鼓 N1	裸 N1	猶 N1
sword, saber, knife	drum, beat, rouse, muster	naked, nude, uncovered, partially clothed	furthermore, still, yet
வாள்	டிரம்	நிர்வாணமாக	மேலும்
塊 N1	旋 N1	弓 N1	幣 N1
clod, lump, chink, clot, mass	rotation, go around	bow, bow (archery, violin)	cash, bad habit, humble prefix, gift
clod	சுழற்சி	வில்	பணம்
膜 N1	扇 N1	腸 N1	槽 N1
membrane	fan, folding fan	intestines, guts, bowels, viscera	vat, tub, tank
சவ்வு	விசிறி	குடல்	வாட்
慈 N1	楊 N1	伐 N1	駿 N1
mercy	willow	fell, strike, attack, punish	a good horse, speed, a fast person
கருணை	வில்லோ	விழுந்தது	வேகம்
糾 N1	亮 N1	墳 N1	坪 N1
twist, ask, investigate, verify	clear, help	tomb, mound	two-mat area, ~36 sq ft
திருப்பம்	தெளிவானது	கல்லறை	இரண்டு பாய் பகுதி

紺 (N1)	娯 (N1)	舌 (N1)	羅 (N1)
dark blue, navy	recreation, pleasure	tongue, reed, clapper	gauze, thin silk, Rome
கடற்படை	பொழுதுபோக்கு	நாக்கு	துணி

峡 (N1)	俸 (N1)	厘 (N1)	峰 (N1)
gorge, ravine	stipend, salary	rin, 1, 10sen, 1, 10bu	summit, peak
பள்ளத்தாக்கு	உதவித்தொகை	துவைக்க	உச்சிமாநாடு

圭 (N1)	醸 (N1)	蓮 (N1)	弔 (N1)
square jewel, corner, angle, edge	brew, cause	lotus	condolences, mourning, funeral
மூலையில்	கஷாயம்	தாமரை	இரங்கல்

乙 (N1)	汁 (N1)	尼 (N1)	遍 (N1)
the latter, duplicate, strange, witty	soup, juice, broth, sap, gravy, pus	nun	everywhere, times, widely, generally
நகல்	சூப்	கன்னியாஸ்திரி	எல்லா இடங்களிலும்

衡 (N1)	薫 (N1)	猟 (N1)	羊 (N1)
equilibrium, measuring rod, scale	send forth fragrance, fragrant, be scented	game-hunting, shooting, game, bag	sheep
சமநிலை	மணம்	படப்பிடிப்பு	ஆடுகள்

N1	N1	N1	N1
款 goodwill, article, section, friendship, collusion நல்லெண்ணம்	**閲** review, inspection, revision விமர்சனம்	**偵** spy உளவு	**喝** hoarse, scold கரடுமுரடான
敢 daring, sad, tragic, pitiful, frail, feeble தைரியமான	**胎** womb, uterus கருவில்	**酵** fermentation நொதித்தல்	**豚** pork, pig பன்றி இறைச்சி
遮 intercept, interrupt, obstruct இடைமறிப்பு	**扉** front door, title page, front page முன் கதவு	**硫** sulphur கந்தகம்	**赦** pardon, forgiveness மன்னிப்பு
窃 stealth, steal, secret, private, hushed திருட்டு	**泡** bubbles, foam, suds, froth குமிழ்கள்	**瑞** congratulations வாழ்த்துக்கள்	**又** or again, furthermore, on the other hand மேலும்
慨 rue, be sad, sigh, lament புலம்பல்	**紡** spinning நூற்பு	**恨** regret, bear a grudge, resentment, malice, hatred வருத்தம்	**肪** obese, fat பருமனான

扶 N1	戯 N1	伍 N1	忌 N1
aid, help, assist	frolic, play, sport	5, 5-man squad, file, line	mourning, abhor, detestable, death anniversary
உதவி	frolic	கோப்பு	துக்கம்

濁 N1	奔 N1	斗 N1	蘭 N1
voiced, uncleanness, wrong, nigori, impurity	bustle, run	Big Dipper, 10 sho (vol), sake dipper	orchid, Holland
குரல் கொடுத்தார்	சலசலப்பு	பொருட்டு டிப்பர்	ஆர்க்கிட்

迅 N1	肖 N1	鉢 N1	朽 N1
swift, fast	resemblance	bowl, rice tub, pot, crown	decay, rot, remain in seclusion
ஸ்விஃப்ட்	ஒற்றுமை	கிண்ணம்	சிதைவு

殻 N1	享 N1	秦 N1	茅 N1
husk, nut shell	receive, undergo, answer (phone), take, get, catch	Manchu dynasty	miscanthus reed
உமி	பெறு	மஞ்சு வம்சம்	மாவோ

藩 N1	沙 N1	輔 N1	媒 N1
clan, enclosure	sand	help	mediator, go-between
குலம்	மணல்	உதவி	மத்தியஸ்தர்

N1	N1	N1	N1
鶏 chicken கோழி	**禅** Zen, silent meditation தியானம்	**嘱** entrust, request, send a message ஒப்படைக்கவும்	**胴** trunk, torso, hull (ship), hub of wheel தண்டு
迭 transfer, alternation பரிமாற்றம்	**挿** insert, put in, graft, wear (sword) செருக	**嵐** storm, tempest புயல்	**椎** oak, mallet ஓக்
絹 silk பட்டு	**陪** obeisance, follow, accompany, attend on வணக்கம்	**剖** divide பிரி	**譜** musical score, music, note, staff, table, genealogy இசை
郁 cultural progress, perfume வாசனை	**悠** permanence, distant, long time, leisure நிரந்தரம்	**淑** graceful, gentle, pure அழகான	**帆** sail பயணம்
暁 daybreak, dawn, in the event பகல்	**傑** greatness, excellence மகத்துவம்	**楠** camphor tree கற்பூரம் மரம்	**笛** flute, clarinet, pipe, whistle, bagpipe, piccolo புல்லாங்குழல்

玲 N1	奴 N1	錠 N1	拳 N1
sound of jewels	guy, slave, manservant, fellow	lock, fetters, shackles	fist
நகைகளின் ஒலி	பையன்	பூட்டு	முஷ்டி
遷 N1	拙 N1	侍 N1	尺 N1
transition, move, change	bungling, clumsy, unskillful	waiter, samurai, wait upon, serve	shaku, Japanese foot, measure, scale, rule
மாற்றம்	bungling	பணியாளர்	அளவு
峠 N1	篤 N1	肇 N1	渇 N1
mountain peak, mountain pass, climax	fervent, kind, cordial, serious, deliberate	beginning	thirst, dry up, parch
க்ளைமாக்ஸ்	ஆர்வமுள்ள	ஆரம்பம்	தாகம்
叔 N1	雌 N1	亨 N1	堪 N1
uncle, youth	feminine, female	undergo, answer (phone), take, get, catch	withstand, endure, support, resist
மாமா	பெண்பால்	உட்பட்டது	தாங்க
叙 N1	酢 N1	吟 N1	遞 N1
confer, relate, narrate, describe	vinegar, sour, acid, tart	versify, singing, recital	relay, in turn, sending
வழங்குதல்	வினிகர்	விவரிக்கவும்	ரிலே

N1	N1	N1	N1
嶺	**甚**	**喬**	**崇**
peak, summit	tremendously, very, great, exceedingly	high, boasting	adore, respect, revere, worship
உச்சம்	மிகப்பெரிய	உயர்	வணங்கு
漆	**岬**	**癖**	**愉**
lacquer, varnish, seven	headland, cape, spit, promontory	mannerism, habit, vice, trait, fault, kink	pleasure, happy, rejoice
அரக்கு	ஹெட்லேண்ட்	நடத்தை	இன்பம்
寅	**礁**	**乃**	**洲**
sign of the tiger, 3-5AM	reef, sunken rock	from, possessive particle, whereupon, accordingly	continent, sandbar, island, country
புலி	ரீஃப்	அதன்படி	கண்டம்
屯	**樺**	**槙**	**姻**
barracks, police station, camp	birch	twig, ornamental evergreen	matrimony, marry
சரமாரியாக	பிர்ச்	கிளை	திருமணம்
巌	**擬**	**塀**	**唇**
rock, crag, boulder	mimic, aim (a gun) at, nominate, imitate	fence, wall, (kokuji)	lips
பாறை	மிமிக்	வேலி	உதடுகள்

<table>
<tr><td>

睦

N1

intimate, friendly, harmonious

நெருக்கமான

</td><td>

閑

N1

leisure

ஓய்வு

</td><td>

胡

N1

barbarian, foreign

காட்டுமிராண்டி

</td><td>

幽

N1

seclude, confine to a room

ஒதுக்கி

</td></tr>
<tr><td>

峻

N1

high, steep

உயர்

</td><td>

曹

N1

cadet, friend

கேடட்

</td><td>

詠

N1

recitation, poem, song, composing

பாராயணம்

</td><td>

卑

N1

lowly, base, vile, vulgar

தாழ்ந்த

</td></tr>
<tr><td>

侮

N1

scorn, despise, make light of, contempt

அவதூறு

</td><td>

鋳

N1

casting, mint

வார்ப்பு

</td><td>

抹

N1

rub, paint, erase

தேய்க்கவும்

</td><td>

尉

N1

military officer, jailer, old man, rank

ஜெயிலர்

</td></tr>
<tr><td>

隷

N1

slave, servant, prisoner, criminal, follower

அடிமை

</td><td>

禍

N1

calamity, misfortune, evil, curse

பேரழிவு

</td><td>

蝶

N1

butterfly

பட்டாம்பூச்சி

</td><td>

酪

N1

dairy products, whey, broth, fruit juice

மோர்

</td></tr>
<tr><td>

茎

N1

stalk, stem

தண்டு

</td><td>

帥

N1

commander, leading troops, governor

தளபதி

</td><td>

逝

N1

departed, die

புறப்பட்டது

</td><td>

汽

N1

vapor, steam

நீராவி

</td></tr>
</table>

琢 N1	**匿** N1	**襟** N1	**蛍** N1
polish	hide, shelter, shield	collar, neck, lapel	lightning-bug, firefly
போலிஷ்	மறை	காலர்	மின்மினிப் பூச்சி
蕉 N1	**寡** N1	**琉** N1	**痢** N1
banana	widow, minority, few	lapis lazuli	diarrhea
வாழை	சிறுபான்மை	lapis lazuli	வயிற்றுப்போக்கு
庸 N1	**朋** N1	**坑** N1	**藍** N1
commonplace, ordinary, employment	companion, friend	pit, hole	indigo
பொதுவான இடம்	துணை	குழி	இண்டிகோ
賊 N1	**搾** N1	**畔** N1	**遼** N1
burglar, rebel, traitor, robber	squeeze	paddy ridge, levee	distant
களவு	கசக்கி	levee	தொலைதூர
唄 N1	**孔** N1	**橘** N1	**漱** N1
songs with samisen	cavity, hole, slit, very, great, exceedingly	mandarin orange	gargle, rinse mouth
பாடல்கள்	குழி	ஆரஞ்சு	கர்ஜனை

N1	N1	N1	N1
呂	**拷**	**嬢**	**苑**
spine, backbone	torture, beat	lass, girl, Miss, daughter	garden, farm, park
முதுகெலும்பு	சித்திரவதை	லாஸ்	தோட்டம்
巽	**杜**	**渓**	**翁**
southeast	woods, grove	mountain stream, valley	venerable old man
தென்கிழக்கு	ஹூட்ஸ்	பள்ளத்தாக்கு	மரியாதைக்குரிய வயதான மனிதன்
廉	**謹**	**瞳**	**湧**
bargain, reason, charge, suspicion	discreet, reverently, humbly	pupil	boil, ferment, seethe, uproar, breed
பேரம்	விவேகமுள்ள	மாணவர்	கொதி
欣	**窯**	**褒**	**醜**
take pleasure in, rejoice	kiln, oven, furnace	praise, extol	ugly, unclean, shame, bad looking
மகிழ்ச்சியுங்கள்	சூளை	புகழ்	அசிங்கமான
升	**煩**	**巴**	**禎**
measuring box, 1.8 liter	anxiety, trouble, worry, pain, ill, annoy	comma-design	happiness
அளவிடும் பெட்டி	கவலை	வடிவமைப்பு	மகிழ்ச்சி

N1	N1	N1	N1
劾	**堕**	**租**	**稜**
censure, criminal investigation	degenerate, descend to, lapse into	tariff, crop tax, borrowing	angle, edge, corner, power, majesty
தணிக்கை	சீரழிவு	சுங்கவரி	கோணம்
栈	**倭**	**婿**	**斐**
scaffold, cleat, frame, jetty, bolt (door)	Yamato, ancient Japan	bridegroom, son-in-law	beautiful, patterned
சாரக்கட்டு	ஜப்பான்	மணமகன்	அழகு
罷	**矯**	**某**	**囚**
quit, stop, leave, withdraw, go	rectify, straighten, correct, reform, cure	so-and-so, one, a certain, that person	captured, criminal, arrest, catch
விட்டுவிட	திருத்து	சில	கைப்பற்றப்பட்டது
魁	**虹**	**鴻**	**泌**
charging ahead of others	rainbow	large bird, wild goose	ooze, flow, soak in, penetrate, secrete
கட்டணம் வசூலிக்கிறது	வானவில்	வாத்து	ஊடுருவி
於	**赳**	**漸**	**蚊**
at, in, on, as for	strong and brave	steadily, gradually advancing, finally, barely	mosquito
இல்	தைரியமான	சீராக	கொசு

葵 N1	厄 N1	藻 N1	禄 N1
hollyhock	unlucky, misfortune, bad luck, disaster	seaweed, duckweed	fief, allowance, pension, grant, happiness
ஹோலிஹாக்	துரதிர்ஷ்டவசமான	கடற்பாசி	fief
孟 N1	嫡 N1	尭 N1	嚇 N1
chief, beginning	legitimate wife, direct descent (non-bastard)	high, far	menacing, dignity, majesty, threaten
தலைமை	மனைவி	உயர்	அச்சுறுத்தல்
凸 N1	暢 N1	韻 N1	霜 N1
convex, beetle brow, uneven	stretch	rhyme, elegance, tone	frost
குவிந்த	நீட்சி	ரைம்	பனி
硝 N1	勅 N1	芹 N1	杏 N1
nitrate, saltpeter	imperial order	parsley	apricot
நைட்ரேட்	ஏகாதிபத்திய ஒழுங்கு	வோக்கோசு	பாதாமி
棺 N1	儒 N1	鳳 N1	馨 N1
coffin, casket	Confucian	male mythical bird	fragrant, balmy, favourable
சவப்பெட்டி	கன்பூசியன்	பறவை	மணம்

慧 N1	愁 N1	楼 N1	彬 N1
wise	distress, grieve, lament, be anxious	watchtower, lookout, high building	refined, gentle
பாண்டித்தியம்	துன்பம்	காவற்கோபுரம்	சுத்திகரிக்கப்பட்டது
匡 N1	眉 N1	欽 N1	薪 N1
correct, save, assist	eyebrow	respect, revere, long for	fuel, firewood, kindling
சரி	புருவம்	மரியாதை	எரிபொருள்
褐 N1	賜 N1	嵯 N1	綜 N1
brown, woollen kimono	grant, gift, boon, results	steep, craggy, rugged	rule
பழுப்பு	மானியம்	செங்குத்தான	ஆட்சி
繕 N1	栓 N1	翠 N1	鮎 N1
darning, repair, mend, trim, tidy up, adjust	plug, bolt, cork, bung, stopper	green	freshwater trout, smelt
எச்சரிக்கை	பிளக்	பச்சை	ஸ்மெல்ட்
榛 N1	凹 N1	艶 N1	惣 N1
hazelnut, filbert	concave, hollow, sunken	glossy, luster, glaze, polish, charm, colorful	all
பழுப்புநிறம்	குழிவான	பளபளப்பான	அனைத்தும்

蔦 N1 vine, ivy கொடியின்	**錬** N1 tempering, refine, drill, train, polish வெப்பநிலை மாற்றம்	**隼** N1 falcon ஃபால்கன்	**渚** N1 strand, beach, shore இழை
衷 N1 inmost, heart, mind, inside பெரும்பாலான	**逐** N1 pursue, drive away, chase, accomplish, attain தொடர	**斥** N1 reject, retreat, recede, withdraw, repel, repulse நிராகரி	**稀** N1 rare, phenomenal, dilute (acid) அரிதானது
芙 N1 lotus, Mt Fuji தாமரை	**皐** N1 swamp, shore சதுப்பு நிலம்	**雛** N1 chick, squab, duckling, doll குஞ்சு	**惟** N1 consider, reflect, think கருத்தில் கொள்ளுங்கள்
佑 N1 help, assist உதவி	**耀** N1 shine, sparkle, gleam, twinkle பிரகாசிக்கவும்	**黛** N1 blackened eyebrows புருவங்கள்	**渥** N1 kindness கருணை
憧 N1 yearn after, long for, aspire to, admire, adore வணங்கு	**宵** N1 wee hours, evening, early night சாயங்காலம்	**妄** N1 delusion, unnecessarily, without authority மாயை	**惇** N1 sincere, kind, considerate நேர்மையான

N1	N1	N1	N1
脩	甫	酌	蚕
dried meat	for the first time, not until	bar-tending, serving sake, the host, draw (water)	silkworm
உலர்ந்த இறைச்சி	முதல் தடவை	பார்-டெண்டிங்	பட்டுப்புழு
嬉	蒼	暉	頒
glad, pleased, rejoice	blue, pale	shine, light	distribute, disseminate, partition, understand
மகிழ்ச்சி	நீலம்	பிரகாசிக்கவும்	விநியோகிக்கவும்
只	肢	檀	凱
only, free, in addition	limb, arms & legs	cedar, sandlewood, spindle tree	victory song
மட்டும்	மூட்டு	சிடார்	வெற்றி பாடல்
彗	嗣	叶	汐
comet	heir, succeed	grant, answer	eventide, tide, salt water, opportunity
வால் நட்சத்திரம்	வாரிசு	மானியம்	நிகழ்வு
絢	朔	伽	畝
kimono design	conjunction (astronomy), first day of month	nursing, attending, entertainer	furrow, 30 tsubo, ridge, rib
கிமோனோ	இணைத்தல்	நர்சிங்	உரோமம்

抄 N1 extract, selection, summary, copy, spread thin பிரித்தெடுத்தல்	**爽** N1 refreshing, bracing, resonant, sweet, clear புத்துணர்ச்சி	**黎** N1 dark, black, many இருள்	**惰** N1 lazy, laziness சோம்பேறி
蛮 N1 barbarian காட்டுமிராண்டி	**冴** N1 be clear, serene, cold, skilful தெளிவாக இருங்கள்	**旺** N1 flourishing, successful, beautiful, vigorous செழித்து வளர்கிறது	**萌** N1 show symptoms of, sprout, bud, malt முளைப்பயிர்
偲 N1 recollect, remember நினைவுகூருங்கள்	**壱** N1 I, one நான்	**瑠** N1 lapis lazuli lapis lazuli	**允** N1 license, sincerity, permit உரிமம்
蒔 N1 sow (seeds) விதைக்க	**鯉** N1 carp கெண்டை	**弧** N1 arc, arch, bow வில்	**遥** N1 far off, distant, long ago தொலைதூர
瑛 N1 sparkle of jewelry, crystal படிக	**附** N1 affixed, attach, refer to, append ஒட்டப்பட்டுள்ளது	**彪** N1 spotted, mottled, patterned, small tiger காணப்பட்டது	**但** N1 however, but எனினும்

N1	N1	N1	N1
綺	芋	茜	凌
figured cloth, beautiful	potato	madder, red dye, Turkey red	endure, keep (rain)out, stave off, tide over
அழகு	உருளைக்கிழங்கு	பைத்தியம்	தாங்க
皓	洸	毬	婆
white, clear	sparkling water	burr, ball	old woman, grandma, wet nurse
வெள்ளை	பிரகாசமான நீர்	பர்	பாட்டி
緋	鯛	怜	邑
scarlet, cardinal	sea bream, red snapper	wise	village, rural community
கருஞ்சிவப்பு	கடல் ப்ரீம்	பாண்டித்தியம்	கிராமம்
倣	碧	啄	穰
emulate, imitate	blue, green	peck, pick up	good crops, prosperity
பின்பற்றவும்	நீலம்	பெக்	செழிப்பு
酉	倹	柚	繭
west, bird, sign of the bird	frugal, economy, thrifty	citron	cocoon
மேற்கு	அளவாக செலவிடுதல்	சிட்ரான்	கூட்டை

N1 亦	N1 詢	N1 采	N1 紗
also, again	consult with	dice, form, appearance, take, coloring	gauze, gossamer
மேலும்	கலந்தாலோசிக்கவும்	பகடை	துணி
N1 賦	N1 眸	N1 玖	N1 弍
levy, ode, prose, poem, tribute, installment	pupil of the eye	beautiful black jewel, nine	two, second
வசூல் செய்தல்	மாணவர்	ஒன்பது	இரண்டு
N1 錘	N1 諄	N1 倖	N1 痘
weight, plumb bob, sinker	tedious	happiness, luck	pox, smallpox
எடை	கடினமான	மகிழ்ச்சி	pox
N1 笙	N1 侃	N1 裟	N1 洵
a reed instrument	strong, just, righteous, peace-loving	Buddhist surplice	alike, truth
ஒரு நாணல் கருவி	வலுவான	ப sur த்த உபரி	ஒரே மாதிரியாக
N1 爾	N1 耗	N1 昴	N1 銑
you, thou, second person	decrease	the Pleiades	pig iron
நீங்கள்	குறைகிறது	பிளேயட்ஸ்	பன்றி இரும்பு

莞 N1	伶 N1	碩 N1	宥 N1
reed used to cover tatami	actor	large, great, eminent	soothe, calm, pacify
நாணல்	நடிகர்	பெரியது	ஆற்றவும்
淏 N1	晏 N1	伎 N1	朕 N1
deep and broad	late, quiet, sets (sun)	deed, skill	majestic plural, imperial we
பரந்த	தாமதமாக	பத்திரம்	கம்பீரமான
迪 N1	綸 N1	且 N1	竣 N1
edify, way, path	thread, silk cloth	moreover, also, furthermore	end, finish
திருத்து	நூல்	மேலும்	முடிவு
晨 N1	吏 N1	燦 N1	麿 N1
morning, early	officer, an official	brilliant	I, you, (kokuji)
காலை	அதிகாரி	புத்திசாலி	நான்
頌 N1	箇 N1	楓 N1	琳 N1
eulogy	counters for things	maple	jewel, tinkling of jewelry
புகழ்	கவுண்டர்கள்	மேப்பிள்	நகை

梧 N1	哉 N1	澪 N1	晟 N1
Chinese parasol tree, phoenix tree	how, what, alas, (question mark)	water route, shipping channel	clear
பீனிக்ஸ் மரம்	எப்படி,	நீர் பாதை	தெளிவானது
衿 N1	凪 N1	梢 N1	丙 N1
neck, collar, lapel	lull, calm, (kokuji)	treetops, twig	third class, 3rd, 3rd calendar sign
கழுத்து	மந்தமான	மரங்கள்	மூன்றாவது
颯 N1	茄 N1	勺 N1	恕 N1
suddenly, smoothly	eggplant	ladle, one tenth of a go, dip	excuse, tolerate, forgive
திடீரென்று	கத்திரிக்காய்	அகப்பை	சாக்குப்போக்கு
瑚 N1	遵 N1	瞭 N1	燎 N1
ancestral offering receptacle	abide by, follow, obey, learn	clear	burn, bonfire
மூதாதையர்	அறிய	தெளிவானது	எரிக்க
虞 N1	柊 N1	侑 N1	謁 N1
uneasiness, fear, anxiety, concern	holly	urge to eat	audience, audience (with king)
சங்கடம்	ஹோலி	சாப்பிட தூண்டுதல்	பார்வையாளர்கள்

斤 N1	**嵩** N1	**捺** N1	**蓉** N1
axe, 1.32 lb, catty, counter for loaves of bread	be aggravated, grow worse, grow bulky, swell	press, print, affix a seal, stamp	lotus
கோடரி	வீக்கம்	முத்திரை	தாமரை
茉 N1	**燿** N1	**誼** N1	**冶** N1
jasmine	shine	friendship, intimacy	melting, smelting
மல்லிகை	பிரகாசிக்கவும்	நட்பு	உருகுதல்
栞 N1	**墾** N1	**勁** N1	**菖** N1
bookmark, guidebook	ground-breaking, open up farmland	strong	iris
புத்தககுறி	விவசாய நிலம்	வலுவான	கருவிழி
椋 N1	**叡** N1	**胤** N1	**凜** N1
type of deciduous tree, grey starling	intelligence, imperial	descendent, issue, offspring	cold, strict, severe
மரம்	உளவுத்துறை	வம்சாவளி	குளிர்
亥 N1	**爵** N1	**脹** N1	**麟** N1
sign of the hog, 9-11PM	baron, peerage, court rank	dilate, distend, bulge, fill out, swell	Chinese unicorn, genius, giraffe, bright, shining
பன்றியின் அடையாளம்	பரோன்	dilate	பிரகாசிக்கிறது

<table>
<tr>
<td>莉
N1

jasmine

மல்லிகை</td>
<td>汰
N1

luxury, select

ஆடம்பர</td>
<td>瑤
N1

beautiful as a jewel

அழகு</td>
<td>瑳
N1

polish

போலிஷ்</td>
</tr>
<tr>
<td>耶
N1

question mark

கேள்வி குறி</td>
<td>椰
N1

coconut tree

தென்னை மரம்</td>
<td>絃
N1

string, cord, samisen music

லேசான கயிறு</td>
<td>丞
N1

help

உதவி</td>
</tr>
<tr>
<td>璃
N1

glassy, lapis lazuli

கண்ணாடி</td>
<td>奎
N1

star, god of literature

நட்சத்திரம்</td>
<td>塑
N1

model, molding

மாதிரி</td>
<td>昂
N1

rise

உயர்வு</td>
</tr>
<tr>
<td>柾
N1

straight grain, spindle tree, (kokuji)

நேராக தானிய</td>
<td>熙
N1

bright, sunny, prosperous, merry

பிரகாசமான</td>
<td>菫
N1

the violet

வயலட்</td>
<td>諒
N1

fact, reality, understand, appreciate

உண்மை</td>
</tr>
<tr>
<td>鞠
N1

ball

பந்து</td>
<td>崚
N1

towering in a row

ஒரு வரிசையில் உயர்ந்தது</td>
<td>濫
N1

excessive, overflow, spread out

அதிகப்படியான</td>
<td>捷
N1

victory, fast

வெற்றி</td>
</tr>
</table>

www.ingramcontent.com/pod-product-compliance
Lightning Source LLC
Chambersburg PA
CBHW080717120726
48001CB00010B/3056